CHARLES VANCE

Heralds of the Almighty

Prophets of the Bible

First published by Mountaintop Publishing 2023

First edition

This book was professionally typeset on Reedsy.
Find out more at reedsy.com

Contents

Preface

The prophets of the Bible have fascinated and inspired people for centuries. Their messages of hope, judgment, and restoration continue to speak to us today, providing guidance, direction, and comfort in times of uncertainty and upheaval.

This book, "Heralds of the Almighty: Prophets of the Bible," is an exploration of the lives and messages of these important figures in the Bible. It is written for readers who want to gain a deeper understanding of the prophets and their role in the history of Israel and the early church.

In these pages, you will find an overview of the major and minor prophets in the Bible, their messages, and the historical and cultural context in which they lived. The book also provides insights into the prophetic tradition, including the unique styles and themes of the prophets, and how their messages can be applied to contemporary issues and challenges.

The goal of this book is to provide readers with a comprehensive and engaging introduction to the prophets of the Bible, and to encourage further study and exploration. Whether you are new to the study of the prophets or a seasoned scholar, I hope that this book will deepen your understanding of these important figures and their messages.

May the words of the prophets inspire us to seek God's will and to live lives of faith, hope, and love.

Sincerely,

Charles Vance

1

Introduction

In the Bible, a prophet is a person who speaks for God and delivers messages or prophecies to the people. The role of a prophet is to convey God's word to the people and to call them to repentance, obedience, and faithfulness. Prophets often spoke about future events, such as judgment or salvation, and sometimes used symbolic language or performed symbolic actions to communicate their messages.

The prophets played a crucial role in the history of Israel and the early Christian church. They served as intermediaries between God and the people, providing guidance, direction, and correction. They also provided hope and encouragement during times of trial and hardship.

In the New Testament, the role of prophets is seen as continuing through the gift of prophecy, which is given by the Holy Spirit to some members of the church. The gift of prophecy is not limited to predicting future events, but also includes speaking God's word and messages to the church for encouragement, edification, and exhortation.

Overall, the role of a prophet in the Bible is to speak for God and to convey his messages to the people in order to guide, direct, and encourage them in their relationship with him.

Major and Minor Prophets

The difference between major and minor prophets in the Bible is primarily based on the length of their books. The five major prophets - Isaiah, Jeremiah, Lamentations, Ezekiel, and Daniel - have books that are longer and more extensive than the books of the twelve minor prophets - Hosea, Joel, Amos, Obadiah, Jonah, Micah, Nahum, Habakkuk, Zephaniah, Haggai, Zechariah, and Malachi.

However, this distinction is not based on the importance or significance of the prophets themselves or their messages. The minor prophets still played important roles in the history of Israel and the early church, and their messages are still relevant and valuable for believers today.

In addition, some scholars suggest that the distinction between major and minor prophets may also relate to the scope and complexity of their messages. The major prophets often address a broad range of theological and social issues, while the minor prophets may focus more narrowly on specific themes or events.

Overall, while the distinction between major and minor prophets is primarily based on the length of their books, both groups of prophets are important and valuable for understanding God's messages to his people in the Bible.

Historical Cultural Context

The historical and cultural context of the prophets is crucial for understanding their messages and their role in the Bible. The prophets lived in a time of great political, social, and religious change, and their messages were shaped by these factors.

In the Old Testament, the prophets lived primarily in the period of the divided kingdom (c. 930-586 BC) and the exile (586-538 BC), which followed the destruction of the southern kingdom of Judah by the Babylonians. During this time, Israel and Judah were ruled by various kings and faced threats from neighboring nations, such as Assyria and Babylon. The prophets spoke out against the political and religious corruption of the rulers and called the people to repentance and faithfulness to God. They warned of impending judgment and exile, but also promised eventual restoration and salvation.

The prophets also addressed the religious and cultural practices of the Israelites. They spoke out against idolatry, false prophets, and social injustice. They emphasized the importance of the law and the worship of God in the temple, but also emphasized the need for sincerity and humility in their relationship with God.

In the New Testament, the prophets lived in the period of the Roman occupation of Israel and the early church (c. 30-100 AD). They spoke out against false teachings and moral corruption within the church and emphasized the importance of unity, love, and faithfulness to God.

Overall, the historical and cultural context of the prophets provides important background for understanding their messages and their significance in the Bible. The prophets spoke to specific situations and issues in their own time, but their messages still have relevance and value for believers today.

Timeline

It is difficult to provide an exact chronological order for the prophets in the Old Testament, as the dating of some of their writings is uncertain and varies among scholars. However, here is a general timeline that places the prophets in their historical context:

1. Obadiah (848-841 BC) - prophesied against the Edomites and their mistreatment of the Israelites.
2. Joel (830-800 BC) - prophesied about a locust plague and called the people to repentance and renewal.
3. Jonah (790-760 BC) - prophesied to the city of Nineveh and called them to repentance.
4. Amos (760-750 BC) - prophesied against the social and religious injustices of the northern kingdom of Israel.
5. Hosea (750-722 BC) - prophesied against the spiritual adultery and unfaithfulness of the northern kingdom of Israel.

6. Isaiah (740-700 BC) - prophesied to the southern kingdom of Judah and spoke about the coming Messiah and the restoration of Israel.
7. Micah (735-700 BC) - prophesied to both the northern and southern kingdoms of Israel and called for justice and righteousness.
8. Nahum (663-612 BC) - prophesied about the fall of Nineveh and the Assyrian empire.
9. Zephaniah (640-609 BC) - prophesied to the southern kingdom of Judah and called for repentance and warned of judgment.
10. Jeremiah (627-586 BC) - prophesied to the southern kingdom of Judah and warned of the Babylonian invasion and exile.
11. Habakkuk (612-589 BC) - prophesied to the southern kingdom of Judah and questioned God about the apparent injustice of his ways.
12. Ezekiel (593-571 BC) - prophesied to the exiles in Babylon and spoke about the restoration and renewal of Israel.
13. Daniel (605-536 BC) - prophesied to the exiles in Babylon and interpreted dreams and visions for the Babylonian kings.
14. Haggai (520 BC) - prophesied to the Jews who had returned from exile and encouraged them to rebuild the temple in Jerusalem.
15. Zechariah (520-518 BC) - prophesied to the Jews who had returned from exile and spoke about the coming Messiah and the restoration of Israel.
16. Malachi (430-400 BC) - prophesied to the Jews who had returned from exile and spoke about the need for faithfulness and the coming of the Messiah.

Again, it should be noted that the exact dating and order of the prophets is not always clear and there may be some variation among scholars.

2

Obadiah - Minor Prophet (848-841 BC)

The name "Obadiah" means "servant of Yahweh" or "worshipper of Yahweh" in Hebrew. It is a combination of the words "Obad" (meaning "servant" or "worshipper") and "Yah" (a shortened form of Yahweh, the Hebrew name for God).

Obadiah was a minor prophet in the Old Testament of the Bible, and little is known about his background or life. The book of Obadiah is the shortest book in the Old Testament, consisting of only 21 verses, and it is primarily concerned with the judgment of the nation of Edom.

Edom was a neighboring nation to Israel, and the two nations had a long and complicated history. According to the Bible, the Edomites were descendants of Esau, the brother of Jacob (Israel), and the two brothers had a contentious relationship that continued between their respective nations. In Obadiah's time, the Edomites were seen as enemies of Israel and were accused of mistreating the Israelites, particularly during times of war and conflict.

Obadiah's prophetic message is a warning of judgment against the Edomites for their mistreatment of the Israelites. He prophesies that the nation will be brought low and destroyed, and that their wealth and power will be taken away. The book of Obadiah ends with a promise of restoration for the nation of Israel, which has suffered at the hands of the Edomites and other neighboring nations.

Historical Cultural Context

The historical and cultural context in which Obadiah lived is not well-documented, but there are a few key details that can be gleaned from his prophetic book in the Bible. Obadiah was a contemporary of other prophets such as Joel, Amos, and Jonah, and is believed to have lived in the 9th century BC or possibly the 6th century BC.

Obadiah's prophetic message is primarily focused on the nation of Edom, which was a neighboring nation to Israel. At the time of Obadiah, the Edomites were seen as enemies of Israel and were accused of mistreating the Israelites, particularly during times of conflict.

In addition to this historical context, there are also some cultural and religious elements that may have influenced Obadiah's message. The Edomites practiced a religion that was similar to that of the Israelites, but with some differences, and it is possible that Obadiah's message was influenced by this religious context. Additionally, the concept of justice and retribution is a recurring theme throughout the book of Obadiah, which may reflect the cultural values of the time.

Overall, the historical and cultural context in which Obadiah lived was one of political and religious tension between the neighboring nations of Israel and Edom, and his prophetic message reflects this context in its focus on judgment and retribution against the Edomites.

Importance

The book of Obadiah, though short, is significant for several reasons:

1. It contains a powerful message of judgment against the nation of Edom for their mistreatment of the Israelites. This message reinforces the idea that God is just and will hold nations accountable for their actions.
2. The book of Obadiah provides a historical record of the conflict between Israel and Edom, shedding light on the political and cultural context of the time.

3. The book of Obadiah also contains a message of hope and restoration for the nation of Israel, which had suffered at the hands of the Edomites and other neighboring nations. This message of hope points forward to the coming of the Messiah and the ultimate restoration of God's people.
4. The book of Obadiah has been used throughout history as a source of inspiration and guidance for believers. Its message of judgment and restoration speaks to the timeless themes of justice and redemption, and its call to repentance and faithfulness is as relevant today as it was in ancient times.

Overall, the book of Obadiah may be short, but its message is powerful and relevant, making it an important part of the prophetic books of the Old Testament.

Structure and Organization

The book of Obadiah is the shortest book in the Old Testament, consisting of only 21 verses. Despite its brevity, the book is structured in a clear and organized way.

The book of Obadiah can be divided into two main sections:

1. Judgment against Edom (verses 1-16) The first section of the book contains a prophetic message of judgment against the nation of Edom. Obadiah prophesies that Edom will be brought low and destroyed, and that their wealth and power will be taken away. The judgment is said to be a result of Edom's mistreatment of the Israelites, particularly during times of war and conflict.
2. Restoration for Israel (verses 17-21) The second section of the book contains a message of hope and restoration for the nation of Israel. Obadiah prophesies that Israel will ultimately triumph over their enemies, including Edom, and that they will possess the land that has been taken from them. The book ends with a promise of deliverance and a declaration of the Lord's sovereignty over all the earth.

Overall, the structure of Obadiah is straightforward and follows a clear progression from judgment to restoration. This structure serves to emphasize the justice and righteousness of God and the ultimate triumph of his people.

Judgment against Edom

Here are some verses from Obadiah in the KJV that show the judgment against Edom:

1. "The pride of thine heart hath deceived thee, thou that dwellest in the clefts of the rock, whose habitation is high; that saith in his heart, Who shall bring me down to the ground?" (Obadiah 1:3)
2. "Shall I not in that day, saith the Lord, even destroy the wise men out of Edom, and understanding out of the mount of Esau?" (Obadiah 1:8)
3. "For the day of the Lord is near upon all the heathen: as thou hast done, it shall be done unto thee: thy reward shall return upon thine own head." (Obadiah 1:15)
4. "For thy violence against thy brother Jacob shame shall cover thee, and thou shalt be cut off for ever." (Obadiah 1:10)
5. "And the house of Jacob shall be a fire, and the house of Joseph a flame, and the house of Esau for stubble, and they shall kindle in them, and devour them; and there shall not be any remaining of the house of Esau; for the Lord hath spoken it." (Obadiah 1:18)

These verses, along with others in the book of Obadiah, demonstrate the prophetic message of judgment against the nation of Edom for their mistreatment of the Israelites. The language is strong and unequivocal, emphasizing the seriousness of the judgment and the righteousness of God.

Restoration for Israel

Here are some verses from Obadiah in the KJV that speak to the restoration of Israel:

1. "And saviours shall come up on mount Zion to judge the mount of Esau; and the kingdom shall be the Lord's." (Obadiah 1:21)
2. "But upon mount Zion shall be deliverance, and there shall be holiness; and the house of Jacob shall possess their possessions." (Obadiah 1:17)
3. "And I will bring back the captives of my people Israel, and they shall build the waste cities, and inhabit them; and they shall plant vineyards, and drink the wine thereof; they shall also make gardens, and eat the fruit of them." (Obadiah 1:19)
4. "And they of the south shall possess the mount of Esau; and they of the plain the Philistines: and they shall possess the fields of Ephraim, and the fields of Samaria: and Benjamin shall possess Gilead." (Obadiah 1:19)

These verses speak to the restoration and deliverance of Israel after their exile and the judgment against Edom. The language is hopeful and optimistic, emphasizing the promises of God for his people and their ultimate triumph over their enemies.

The promise of deliverance and the restoration of Israel are key themes throughout the book of Obadiah, and these verses are just a few examples of the prophetic message of hope and restoration contained in the book.

3

Joel - Minor Prophet (830-800 BC)

The name "Joel" means "Yahweh is God" in Hebrew. It is a combination of the words "Yah" (a shortened form of Yahweh, the Hebrew name for God) and "El" (the Hebrew word for God).

The prophet Joel is one of the minor prophets in the Old Testament of the Bible. Not much is known about Joel's background or personal life, but his prophetic message has been preserved in the book that bears his name.

The book of Joel does not provide any specific historical context for the prophet or his message, and scholars disagree on the precise time period in which he lived and prophesied. However, some scholars believe that Joel may have lived during the reign of King Joash of Judah, who ruled from 835-796 BC.

Despite the lack of biographical information about Joel, his prophetic message has been regarded as a powerful and impactful message of judgment, repentance, and restoration. The book of Joel contains vivid and poetic descriptions of a locust plague that devastates the land, as well as warnings of a greater judgment to come if the people do not turn back to God.

Throughout the book, Joel calls the people to repentance and renewal, urging them to turn away from their sin and back to God. He also prophesies about a future day of judgment and restoration, in which God will pour out his Spirit on all people and bring about a new age of blessing and abundance.

Overall, Joel's message emphasizes the importance of faithfulness and obedience to God, the danger of sin and judgment, and the hope of restoration and renewal for those who turn back to God.

Historical and Cultural Context

Assuming Joel prophesied during the reign of King Joash of Judah, who ruled from 835-796 BC, the kingdom of Judah was experiencing relative stability and prosperity under the leadership of King Joash. However, the kingdom was also facing threats from neighboring nations, including the kingdom of Israel to the north and the rising power of Assyria to the east.

In addition to external threats, the kingdom of Judah was also facing internal challenges. The religious reforms instituted by King Jehoshaphat, Joash's predecessor, had not been fully successful in rooting out idolatry and ensuring the faithful worship of Yahweh.

This context of relative stability and prosperity, but also potential danger and spiritual apathy, would have provided a relevant and urgent backdrop for Joel's prophetic message. The locust plague described in the book of Joel may have been a metaphorical representation of the various crises and challenges facing the kingdom of Judah at the time, including the threat of invasion and military defeat, social and economic unrest, and spiritual apathy and disobedience.

Joel's message of judgment and repentance would have been particularly relevant and urgent in this context, emphasizing the need for the people of Judah to turn back to Yahweh and renew their faithfulness and obedience. The calls for fasting, prayer, and the restoration of the temple would have resonated with the religious beliefs and practices of the Israelites at the time.

Overall, while the precise historical and cultural context of Joel's prophetic message remains somewhat uncertain, if we assume that he lived during the reign of King Joash, we can contextualize his message within the broader historical and cultural context of the kingdom of Judah during this time period.

Importance

The book of Joel is important in the Bible for several reasons:

1. Prophetic Message: The book of Joel contains a prophetic message of judgment, repentance, and restoration. Joel's vivid and poetic descriptions of the locust plague and warnings of greater judgment to come call the people of Israel to repentance and renewal, emphasizing the importance of faithfulness and obedience to God.
2. Messianic Prophecy: The book of Joel contains several messianic prophecies, including the promise that God will pour out his Spirit on all people, and the declaration that "everyone who calls on the name of the Lord will be saved" (Joel 2:32). These prophecies were ultimately fulfilled in the coming of Jesus Christ and the establishment of the Church.
3. Eschatological Significance: The book of Joel also has eschatological significance, as many of its prophecies are seen as being fulfilled in the end times. For example, the locust plague and other disasters described in the book are often interpreted as being symbolic of the tribulations and judgments that will come before the return of Christ.
4. Theological Themes: The book of Joel contains several important theological themes, including the sovereignty of God, the danger of sin and judgment, the importance of repentance and renewal, and the hope of salvation and restoration. These themes are central to the message of the Bible as a whole and have important implications for Christian theology and practice.

Overall, the book of Joel is an important prophetic work that emphasizes the urgency of repentance and the hope of restoration and salvation through faithfulness to God. Its messianic prophecies and eschatological significance also make it a key text for understanding the broader theological narrative of the Bible.

Structure and Organization

The book of Joel is structured in a relatively simple and straightforward way. It consists of three chapters, each of which contains a distinct prophetic message.

Chapter 1 describes a devastating locust plague that has ravaged the land of Judah. Joel uses vivid and poetic language to describe the destruction caused by the locusts, and calls the people to mourn and lament the loss of their crops and livelihoods. He also warns of a greater judgment to come if the people do not turn back to God.

Chapter 2 continues the theme of judgment and repentance, but also introduces a message of hope and restoration. Joel describes a future day of judgment in which God will pour out his Spirit on all people, bringing about a time of blessing and abundance. He also calls the people to repent and return to God, promising that if they do, they will be spared from the judgment to come.

Chapter 3 shifts the focus to the nations surrounding Judah, and describes a future judgment in which God will gather all the nations for a final battle. Joel prophesies that God will be victorious and that the people of Judah will be restored and blessed in the aftermath of this great battle.

Overall, the structure of Joel is relatively simple and follows a clear narrative arc. The book begins with a description of judgment and disaster, continues with a call to repentance and renewal, and ends with a message of hope and restoration. The book's emphasis on judgment, repentance, and restoration, as well as its prophetic language and vivid imagery, make it a powerful and impactful work of prophetic literature.

Major Themes

The book of Joel contains several major themes and messages, including:

1. Judgment and Repentance: The book of Joel begins with a description of a locust plague that has devastated the land of Judah, serving as a symbol

of God's judgment on the people for their sins. Joel calls the people to mourn and lament the loss of their crops and livelihoods, and warns of a greater judgment to come if the people do not turn back to God.

2. Restoration and Renewal: While the book of Joel begins with a message of judgment and disaster, it ends with a message of hope and restoration. Joel prophesies that God will pour out his Spirit on all people, bringing about a time of blessing and abundance, and he calls the people to repent and return to God in order to be spared from the judgment to come.
3. The Sovereignty of God: The book of Joel emphasizes the sovereignty and power of God, who is in control of all things and who is the ultimate judge of the nations. Joel's vivid and poetic descriptions of the locust plague and other disasters serve to highlight God's power and authority over all creation.
4. Messianic Prophecy: The book of Joel contains several messianic prophecies, including the promise that God will pour out his Spirit on all people, and the declaration that "everyone who calls on the name of the Lord will be saved" (Joel 2:32). These prophecies were ultimately fulfilled in the coming of Jesus Christ and the establishment of the Church.
5. The Importance of Repentance and Obedience: Throughout the book of Joel, the importance of repentance and obedience to God is emphasized. Joel calls the people to turn away from their sin and to return to God, promising that if they do, they will be spared from the judgment to come.

Overall, the major themes and messages of Joel center around the themes of judgment, repentance, restoration, and the sovereignty and power of God. The book's prophetic language and vivid imagery serve to convey these themes in a powerful and impactful way.

Judgment and Repentance

Here are some verses from Joel in the KJV that deal with the themes of judgment and repentance:

- "Alas for the day! for the day of the LORD is at hand, and as a destruction from the Almighty shall it come." (Joel 1:15)
- "Therefore also now, saith the LORD, turn ye even to me with all your heart, and with fasting, and with weeping, and with mourning: And rend your heart, and not your garments, and turn unto the LORD your God: for he is gracious and merciful, slow to anger, and of great kindness, and repenteth him of the evil." (Joel 2:12-13)
- "Blow ye the trumpet in Zion, and sound an alarm in my holy mountain: let all the inhabitants of the land tremble: for the day of the LORD cometh, for it is nigh at hand." (Joel 2:1)
- "Therefore also now, saith the LORD, turn ye even to me with all your heart, and with fasting, and with weeping, and with mourning: And rend your heart, and not your garments, and turn unto the LORD your God: for he is gracious and merciful, slow to anger, and of great kindness, and repenteth him of the evil." (Joel 2:12-13)
- "Multitudes, multitudes in the valley of decision: for the day of the LORD is near in the valley of decision." (Joel 3:14)

These verses emphasize the urgency of repentance and the consequences of disobedience and sin. They call the people of Judah to turn back to God and to seek his mercy and forgiveness before the day of judgment comes.

Restoration and Renewal

Here are some verses from Joel in the KJV that deal with the themes of restoration and renewal:

- "And I will restore to you the years that the locust hath eaten, the cankerworm, and the caterpiller, and the palmerworm, my great army which I sent among you." (Joel 2:25)
- "And it shall come to pass afterward, that I will pour out my spirit upon all flesh; and your sons and your daughters shall prophesy, your old men shall dream dreams, your young men shall see visions." (Joel 2:28)

- "And it shall come to pass, that whosoever shall call on the name of the LORD shall be delivered: for in mount Zion and in Jerusalem shall be deliverance, as the LORD hath said, and in the remnant whom the LORD shall call." (Joel 2:32)
- "So shall ye know that I am the LORD your God dwelling in Zion, my holy mountain: then shall Jerusalem be holy, and there shall no strangers pass through her any more." (Joel 3:17)
- "And it shall come to pass in that day, that the mountains shall drop down new wine, and the hills shall flow with milk, and all the rivers of Judah shall flow with waters, and a fountain shall come forth of the house of the LORD, and shall water the valley of Shittim." (Joel 3:18)

These verses emphasize the promise of restoration and renewal that God offers to his people. Joel speaks of God's willingness to restore the years that were lost to the locust plague, and of the outpouring of his Spirit upon all flesh. He also promises that whoever calls upon the name of the Lord will be delivered, and that Jerusalem will be made holy once again. These verses offer hope and encouragement to the people of Judah, emphasizing the importance of turning back to God in repentance and seeking his mercy and forgiveness.

The Sovereignty of God

Here are some verses from Joel in the KJV that deal with the theme of the sovereignty of God:

- "The LORD also shall roar out of Zion, and utter his voice from Jerusalem; and the heavens and the earth shall shake: but the LORD will be the hope of his people, and the strength of the children of Israel." (Joel 3:16)
- "The LORD will be terrible unto them: for he will famish all the gods of the earth; and men shall worship him, every one from his place, even all the isles of the heathen." (Joel 2:11)
- "The LORD shall utter his voice before his army: for his camp is very great: for he is strong that executeth his word: for the day of the LORD is great

and very terrible; and who can abide it?" (Joel 2:11)

- "Therefore also now, saith the LORD, turn ye even to me with all your heart, and with fasting, and with weeping, and with mourning: And rend your heart, and not your garments, and turn unto the LORD your God: for he is gracious and merciful, slow to anger, and of great kindness, and repenteth him of the evil." (Joel 2:12–13)

These verses emphasize the sovereignty and power of God over all creation. Joel speaks of God's ability to shake the heavens and the earth, and of his strength in executing his word. He also calls the people of Judah to turn back to God in repentance, reminding them of God's gracious and merciful nature. These verses serve as a reminder that God is in control of all things, and that his sovereignty is a central aspect of his character.

Messianic Prophecy

Here are some verses from Joel in the KJV that contain Messianic prophecy:

- "And it shall come to pass afterward, that I will pour out my spirit upon all flesh; and your sons and your daughters shall prophesy, your old men shall dream dreams, your young men shall see visions: And also upon the servants and upon the handmaids in those days will I pour out my spirit." (Joel 2:28–29)
- "And it shall come to pass, that whosoever shall call on the name of the LORD shall be delivered: for in mount Zion and in Jerusalem shall be deliverance, as the LORD hath said, and in the remnant whom the LORD shall call." (Joel 2:32)
- "And the LORD shall utter his voice before his army: for his camp is very great: for he is strong that executeth his word: for the day of the LORD is great and very terrible; and who can abide it?" (Joel 2:11)
- "So shall ye know that I am the LORD your God dwelling in Zion, my holy mountain: then shall Jerusalem be holy, and there shall no strangers pass through her any more." (Joel 3:17)

These verses contain Messianic prophecy and speak of the coming of the Holy Spirit and the deliverance that will come through the Lord. The pouring out of the Holy Spirit on all flesh was fulfilled on the day of Pentecost in the book of Acts, and the promise that whoever calls on the name of the Lord will be delivered is a reference to the salvation that is available through Jesus Christ. The prophecy that Jerusalem will be holy and no strangers will pass through her anymore speaks of the future restoration of Jerusalem in the Messianic Kingdom. These verses demonstrate the continuity and consistency of God's plan of salvation throughout the Old and New Testaments.

The Importance of Repentance and Obedience

Here are some verses from Joel in the KJV that emphasize the importance of repentance and obedience:

- "Therefore also now, saith the LORD, turn ye even to me with all your heart, and with fasting, and with weeping, and with mourning: And rend your heart, and not your garments, and turn unto the LORD your God: for he is gracious and merciful, slow to anger, and of great kindness, and repenteth him of the evil." (Joel 2:12-13)
- "Blow the trumpet in Zion, sanctify a fast, call a solemn assembly: Gather the people, sanctify the congregation, assemble the elders, gather the children, and those that suck the breasts: let the bridegroom go forth of his chamber, and the bride out of her closet. Let the priests, the ministers of the LORD, weep between the porch and the altar, and let them say, Spare thy people, O LORD, and give not thine heritage to reproach, that the heathen should rule over them: wherefore should they say among the people, Where is their God?" (Joel 2:15-17)
- "Therefore also now, saith the LORD, turn ye even to me with all your heart, and with fasting, and with weeping, and with mourning: And rend your heart, and not your garments, and turn unto the LORD your God: for he is gracious and merciful, slow to anger, and of great kindness, and repenteth him of the evil." (Joel 2:12-13)

- "Multitudes, multitudes in the valley of decision: for the day of the LORD is near in the valley of decision. The sun and the moon shall be darkened, and the stars shall withdraw their shining. The LORD also shall roar out of Zion, and utter his voice from Jerusalem; and the heavens and the earth shall shake: but the LORD will be the hope of his people, and the strength of the children of Israel." (Joel 3:14-16)

These verses emphasize the importance of repentance and obedience to God's commands. Joel calls on the people of Judah to turn to God with all their heart, and to demonstrate their repentance through fasting, weeping, and mourning. The passage also stresses the importance of obedience to God's commands, and of calling on the Lord for mercy and forgiveness. The prophet warns that the day of the Lord is near, and that God will judge those who refuse to repent and turn to Him. These verses highlight the importance of living a life of obedience and faithfulness to God, and of seeking his mercy and forgiveness through repentance.

Army of the Lord

Joel speaks of an army in several places in his book, including in the following verses:

- "Blow ye the trumpet in Zion, and sound an alarm in my holy mountain: let all the inhabitants of the land tremble: for the day of the LORD cometh, for it is nigh at hand; A day of darkness and of gloominess, a day of clouds and of thick darkness, as the morning spread upon the mountains: a great people and a strong; there hath not been ever the like, neither shall be any more after it, even to the years of many generations." (Joel 2:1-2)
- "And the LORD shall utter his voice before his army: for his camp is very great: for he is strong that executeth his word: for the day of the LORD is great and very terrible; and who can abide it?" (Joel 2:11)

These verses describe a powerful and fearsome army that is associated with the day of the Lord. This army is said to be like no other, and it brings darkness, gloominess, and thick clouds with it. Joel also describes God's army, which is very great and strong, and is associated with the day of the Lord as well. This army executes God's word and is a sign of his sovereignty and power over all creation. Overall, the army in Joel's book is a symbol of God's judgment and his ultimate triumph over evil.

4

Jonah - Minor Prophet (790-760 BC)

The name "Jonah" means "dove" in Hebrew. It is derived from the Hebrew word "yonah". The dove was a symbol of peace and innocence in ancient Near Eastern cultures, and it is possible that the name Jonah was given to express these qualities.

Jonah was a prophet in the Old Testament who is best known for his reluctant mission to the city of Nineveh. Very little is known about his background, but according to the book of Jonah, he was the son of Amittai and was from the town of Gath Hepher in the region of Galilee.

Jonah is believed to have prophesied during the reign of Jeroboam II, who ruled the northern kingdom of Israel from around 793-753 BC. At this time, Israel was a powerful and prosperous nation, but it was also marked by social and religious corruption.

According to the book of 2 Kings, Jeroboam II was able to expand Israel's borders and secure its wealth and power, but he did not turn away from the sins of his predecessors. It was during this time that Jonah was called by God to deliver a message of warning and repentance to the people of Nineveh, the capital of Assyria, which was a powerful enemy of Israel.

Despite his initial reluctance and attempts to flee from God, Jonah eventually fulfilled his mission and preached to the people of Nineveh, who repented and turned to God. Jonah's story is a powerful testament to the grace and mercy of God, and it illustrates the importance of obedience and repentance in the life of a believer.

Historical and Cultural Context

Jonah lived during a period of Israel's history when the northern kingdom was marked by social and religious corruption. According to the book of Jonah, he was called by God to deliver a message of warning and repentance to the city of Nineveh, the capital of the Assyrian Empire, which was a powerful and aggressive force in the ancient Near East.

The Assyrians had been expanding their empire for several centuries prior to Jonah's mission, and they eventually became a major threat to Israel and other neighboring kingdoms. The Assyrians were known for their cruelty and violence, and they often used brutal tactics to subdue their enemies. It is possible that some Israelites had been taken captive and resettled in Nineveh, although the biblical text does not provide any specific information on this matter.

Despite the Assyrians' reputation for violence and aggression, Jonah was sent to preach a message of warning and repentance to the people of Nineveh. This message was a call for them to turn away from their wickedness and to seek the mercy and forgiveness of God. While Jonah initially resisted this mission, he eventually fulfilled it, and the people of Nineveh responded by repenting and turning to God.

The historical and cultural context in which Jonah lived was marked by political upheaval and military conflict, as well as by religious and moral decay. Despite these challenges, Jonah's story is a powerful reminder of the grace and mercy of God, and it illustrates the importance of obedience and repentance in the life of a believer.

Importance

The book of Jonah is an important part of the Old Testament and the Bible as a whole for several reasons. First, it provides a powerful example of God's grace and mercy, even toward those who are considered enemies of Israel.

The story of Jonah shows that God desires all people to come to repentance and to be saved, regardless of their nationality, ethnicity, or past actions.

Second, the book of Jonah highlights the importance of obedience and repentance in the life of a believer. Jonah initially resists God's call to preach to the people of Nineveh, but he eventually realizes the error of his ways and fulfills his mission. This story serves as a reminder that we must always be open to God's leading in our lives and be willing to repent when we fall short.

Third, the book of Jonah provides a unique perspective on prophecy and the role of a prophet in the ancient Near East. Unlike many other prophetic books, Jonah does not contain long speeches or detailed predictions of future events. Instead, it tells the story of a prophet who is sent on a mission that seems to have little to do with the fate of Israel itself. This emphasizes the fact that God's message of repentance and salvation is not limited to one particular group or nation.

Fourth, the book of Jonah is an excellent example of storytelling and literary craftsmanship. The narrative is filled with vivid and memorable images, such as the great fish that swallows Jonah, the withered plant that provides shade, and the angry wind and waves that threaten to sink the ship. These images serve to convey the message of the story in a powerful and memorable way, and they have captivated readers and listeners for thousands of years.

Finally, the book of Jonah is referenced by Jesus as a sign of his own authenticity and as a foreshadowing of his death and resurrection. In Matthew 12:39-40, Jesus says that "none will be given it except the sign of the prophet Jonah. For as Jonah was three days and three nights in the belly of a huge fish, so the Son of Man will be three days and three nights in the heart of the earth." By citing the story of Jonah, Jesus was emphasizing the miraculous nature of his own death and resurrection, which is the ultimate sign of his divine authority and power. This reference underscores the central role of Jesus' death and resurrection adding to the enduring significance of Jonah's story.

Structure and Organization

The book of Jonah is organized into four chapters, which together tell the story of Jonah's mission to Nineveh and his subsequent encounter with God.

Chapter 1 begins with God calling Jonah to preach to the people of Nineveh, a city known for its wickedness and violence. Instead of obeying God, however, Jonah flees in the opposite direction, boarding a ship bound for Tarshish.

In Chapter 2, Jonah is thrown overboard during a great storm and swallowed by a great fish. He spends three days and three nights in the fish's belly, where he prays to God for deliverance.

Chapter 3 sees Jonah finally obeying God's command and traveling to Nineveh to preach to the people there. To his surprise, the people of Nineveh repent and turn to God, and God relents from his planned destruction of the city.

Chapter 4 concludes the book with Jonah's reaction to God's mercy toward the people of Nineveh. Jonah becomes angry and bitter, complaining to God that he knew all along that God would be merciful. God responds by teaching Jonah a lesson about compassion and the value of all human life.

The book of Jonah is a tightly structured narrative that is skillfully woven together to convey its themes and messages. The different episodes in the story build upon each other, and the book as a whole is a powerful testimony to the transformative power of repentance, obedience, and mercy.

Major Themes

The book of Jonah contains several major themes that are central to its message.

1. God's sovereignty and mercy: The book of Jonah emphasizes the sovereignty and mercy of God, who is shown to be in control of all events and who desires to extend his mercy even to the wicked people of Nineveh.
2. Repentance and obedience: Jonah's story serves as a reminder of the

importance of repentance and obedience in the life of a believer. Jonah initially resists God's call to preach to the people of Nineveh, but he eventually realizes the error of his ways and fulfills his mission.

3. The universality of God's message: The book of Jonah underscores the fact that God's message of repentance and salvation is not limited to one particular group or nation. The people of Nineveh, who are not part of Israel or Judah, are shown to be responsive to God's message and are ultimately spared from destruction.
4. The power of prayer: Jonah's prayer from the belly of the fish is a powerful testimony to the transformative power of prayer and the faithfulness of God to answer the prayers of his people.
5. The importance of compassion and mercy: The book of Jonah concludes with a powerful message about the importance of compassion and mercy, even toward those who are considered enemies. Jonah's anger and bitterness toward the people of Nineveh is contrasted with God's compassion for them, and the book serves as a reminder of the value of all human life in the eyes of God.

God's sovereignty and mercy

Here are some verses from the book of Jonah that highlight God's sovereignty and mercy, in the King James Version:

1. Jonah 1:3 - "But Jonah rose up to flee unto Tarshish from the presence of the Lord, and went down to Joppa; and he found a ship going to Tarshish: so he paid the fare thereof, and went down into it, to go with them unto Tarshish from the presence of the Lord."
2. Jonah 1:17 - "Now the Lord had prepared a great fish to swallow up Jonah. And Jonah was in the belly of the fish three days and three nights."
3. Jonah 2:7 - "When my soul fainted within me I remembered the Lord: and my prayer came in unto thee, into thine holy temple."
4. Jonah 3:5 - "So the people of Nineveh believed God, and proclaimed a fast, and put on sackcloth, from the greatest of them even to the least of

them."

5. Jonah 4:10-11 - "Then said the Lord, Thou hast had pity on the gourd, for the which thou hast not laboured, neither madest it grow; which came up in a night, and perished in a night: And should not I spare Nineveh, that great city, wherein are more than sixscore thousand persons that cannot discern between their right hand and their left hand; and also much cattle?"

These verses demonstrate God's power to control events, his willingness to extend mercy and forgiveness, and his concern for all people, even those who are not part of Israel or Judah.

Repentance and obedience

Here are some verses from the book of Jonah that emphasize the importance of repentance and obedience, in the King James Version:

1. Jonah 1:2 - "Arise, go to Nineveh, that great city, and cry against it; for their wickedness is come up before me."
2. Jonah 1:3 - "But Jonah rose up to flee unto Tarshish from the presence of the Lord, and went down to Joppa; and he found a ship going to Tarshish: so he paid the fare thereof, and went down into it, to go with them unto Tarshish from the presence of the Lord."
3. Jonah 2:9 - "But I will sacrifice unto thee with the voice of thanksgiving; I will pay that that I have vowed. Salvation is of the Lord."
4. Jonah 3:4 - "And Jonah began to enter into the city a day's journey, and he cried, and said, Yet forty days, and Nineveh shall be overthrown."
5. Jonah 3:10 - "And God saw their works, that they turned from their evil way; and God repented of the evil, that he had said that he would do unto them; and he did it not."

These verses demonstrate the importance of following God's commands, even when they may be difficult or uncomfortable. They also emphasize the need for repentance and turning away from sinful behavior, as well as the transformative power of obedience to God's will.

The universality of God's message

Here are some verses from the book of Jonah that highlight the universality of God's message, in the King James Version:

1. Jonah 1:2 - "Arise, go to Nineveh, that great city, and cry against it; for their wickedness is come up before me."
2. Jonah 3:5 - "So the people of Nineveh believed God, and proclaimed a fast, and put on sackcloth, from the greatest of them even to the least of them."
3. Jonah 4:2 - "And he prayed unto the Lord, and said, I pray thee, O Lord, was not this my saying, when I was yet in my country? Therefore I fled before unto Tarshish: for I knew that thou art a gracious God, and merciful, slow to anger, and of great kindness, and repentest thee of the evil."
4. Jonah 4:11 - "And should not I spare Nineveh, that great city, wherein are more than sixscore thousand persons that cannot discern between their right hand and their left hand; and also much cattle?"

These verses demonstrate that God's message of repentance and salvation is not limited to one particular group or nation, but is intended for all people. The people of Nineveh, who were not part of Israel or Judah, are shown to be responsive to God's message and are ultimately spared from destruction. The book of Jonah serves as a reminder that God's love and mercy are available to all who seek him, regardless of their background or nationality.

The power of prayer

Here are some verses from the book of Jonah that emphasize the power of prayer, in the King James Version:

1. Jonah 1:6 - "So the shipmaster came to him, and said unto him, What meanest thou, O sleeper? arise, call upon thy God, if so be that God will think upon us, that we perish not."
2. Jonah 2:1 - "Then Jonah prayed unto the Lord his God out of the fish's belly,"
3. Jonah 2:2 - "And said, I cried by reason of mine affliction unto the Lord, and he heard me; out of the belly of hell cried I, and thou heardest my voice."
4. Jonah 2:7 - "When my soul fainted within me I remembered the Lord: and my prayer came in unto thee, into thine holy temple."
5. Jonah 4:2 - "And he prayed unto the Lord, and said, I pray thee, O Lord, was not this my saying, when I was yet in my country? Therefore I fled before unto Tarshish: for I knew that thou art a gracious God, and merciful, slow to anger, and of great kindness, and repentest thee of the evil."

These verses demonstrate the power of prayer to connect with God and receive help in times of distress. Even in the midst of his disobedience and rebellion, Jonah turns to prayer for comfort and guidance, and is ultimately shown mercy and forgiveness by God. The book of Jonah reminds us that prayer is a powerful tool for seeking God's will and experiencing his love and grace in our lives.

The importance of compassion and mercy

Here are some verses from the book of Jonah that highlight the importance of compassion and mercy, in the King James Version:

1. Jonah 1:14 - "Wherefore they cried unto the Lord, and said, We beseech thee, O Lord, we beseech thee, let us not perish for this man's life, and lay not upon us innocent blood: for thou, O Lord, hast done as it pleased thee."
2. Jonah 3:9-10 - "Who can tell if God will turn and repent, and turn away from his fierce anger, that we perish not? And God saw their works, that they turned from their evil way; and God repented of the evil, that he had said that he would do unto them; and he did it not."
3. Jonah 4:2 - "And he prayed unto the Lord, and said, I pray thee, O Lord, was not this my saying, when I was yet in my country? Therefore I fled before unto Tarshish: for I knew that thou art a gracious God, and merciful, slow to anger, and of great kindness, and repentest thee of the evil."
4. Jonah 4:11 - "And should not I spare Nineveh, that great city, wherein are more than sixscore thousand persons that cannot discern between their right hand and their left hand; and also much cattle?"

These verses show that compassion and mercy are important aspects of God's character and should be reflected in the attitudes and actions of his followers. In the first verse, the sailors on Jonah's ship plead for mercy and compassion from God to spare their lives. In the second verse, the people of Nineveh demonstrate true repentance and are ultimately spared from destruction. Jonah himself acknowledges God's mercy and kindness in the third verse, and in the final verse, God's concern for even the animals in Nineveh shows the depth of his compassion. The book of Jonah serves as a reminder that God's love extends to all people, and that we should strive to show compassion and mercy to others as well.

5

Amos - Minor Prophet(760-750 BC)

The name "Amos" means "burden-bearer" or "burdened" in Hebrew. It is derived from the Hebrew word "amas", which means "to lift" or "to carry a load". The name may have been given to express the burden or responsibility that Amos felt in delivering his prophetic message to the people of Israel.

Amos was a prophet in the northern kingdom of Israel during the 8th century BC. He was a shepherd and a farmer from the town of Tekoa in Judah before being called by God to prophesy to the people of Israel. Amos is considered one of the twelve minor prophets in the Hebrew Bible.

Amos was an outspoken critic of the social and religious injustices that were prevalent in Israel at the time. He condemned the wealthy for their greed and exploitation of the poor, and spoke out against the false worship and religious rituals that had become prevalent. He warned of impending judgment and called for repentance and renewal.

Despite his humble background, Amos was a powerful and persuasive speaker who challenged the religious and political leaders of his time. His message was a call to justice and righteousness, and his words continue to resonate with readers today.

Historical and Cultural Context

Amos lived during a time of political and social instability in the northern kingdom of Israel. The kingdom had experienced a period of relative prosperity and expansion under the reign of King Jeroboam II, but this was also marked by widespread corruption, social injustice, and religious syncretism.

The wealthy elite had amassed great wealth at the expense of the poor, and many people had become disillusioned with the religious institutions and practices of the time. The worship of the golden calf had become popular, and people were also incorporating elements of Canaanite religion into their practices.

It was in this context that Amos was called by God to prophesy to the people of Israel. He was a shepherd and a farmer from Judah, but he traveled to the northern kingdom to deliver his message of judgment and warning. Amos challenged the religious and political leaders of the time, calling for repentance and a return to true worship of God. He also spoke out against the social injustices and exploitation of the poor that had become rampant in Israel.

Despite the resistance and persecution he faced, Amos continued to deliver his message, warning of the impending judgment that would come as a result of Israel's disobedience and unfaithfulness. His message was a call to renewal and restoration, and his words continue to challenge readers today to examine their own lives and work towards justice and righteousness.

Importance

The book of Amos is significant in the Bible for several reasons. First, it provides a powerful critique of the social and religious conditions of ancient Israel. Amos was a prophet who spoke out against the corruption, injustice, and false worship that had become prevalent in Israel. His message was a call to repentance and renewal, and his words continue to challenge readers to examine their own lives and work towards justice and righteousness.

Second, the book of Amos also contains some of the most memorable and powerful passages in the Old Testament. Amos used vivid imagery and poetic language to convey his message, and his words continue to resonate with readers today.

Third, the book of Amos is significant because it challenges us to consider our own responsibility for social justice and caring for the poor and marginalized. Amos spoke out against the exploitation of the poor and the accumulation of wealth by the rich, and his words challenge us to consider our own attitudes towards wealth and power.

Finally, the book of Amos also contains a message of hope and restoration. Despite the impending judgment that Amos prophesied, he also spoke of the coming of the Messiah and the restoration of Israel. His words remind us that God is a God of justice and mercy, and that he ultimately desires to restore and renew his people.

Structure and Organization

The book of Amos is structured into nine chapters, and can be divided into three main sections:

1. The Prophecies Against the Nations (chapters 1-2): In this section, Amos delivers prophecies of judgment against the surrounding nations, including Damascus, Gaza, Tyre, Edom, Ammon, and Moab. These nations are all condemned for their various sins and injustices.
2. The Prophecies Against Israel (chapters 3-6): In this section, Amos turns his attention to the northern kingdom of Israel. He begins by declaring that Israel will be held accountable for their disobedience and unfaithfulness, and then goes on to list a series of specific sins that the people have committed. He also denounces the religious practices and rituals that have become empty and meaningless.
3. The Vision of Restoration (chapters 7-9): In this final section, Amos receives a series of visions that depict the coming judgment and restoration of Israel. He sees God holding a plumb line to measure the people, and declares that they have been found wanting. However, he also sees a

vision of God standing beside an altar, promising to restore the fortunes of Israel and to bring about a time of peace and prosperity.

Overall, the structure of Amos is marked by a clear progression from judgment to restoration. The book begins with prophecies of judgment against the surrounding nations, moves on to denounce the sins of Israel, and concludes with a message of hope and restoration.

Major themes

The book of Amos contains several major themes, including:

1. The Judgment of God: Amos delivers a message of judgment to the people of Israel, warning them of the consequences of their disobedience and unfaithfulness. He emphasizes that God is a just God who will not overlook sin and that there will be consequences for the people's actions.
2. Social Injustice: Amos denounces the social injustices that were prevalent in Israel during his time. He speaks out against the exploitation of the poor by the wealthy, the corruption of the legal system, and the abuse of power by the ruling elite.
3. False Worship: Amos condemns the religious practices and rituals that have become empty and meaningless. He denounces the worship of false gods, the use of instruments and music in worship, and the neglect of true righteousness and justice.
4. The Sovereignty of God: Amos emphasizes the sovereignty of God and his power over all creation. He declares that God is in control of all things and that his judgment is inevitable.
5. The Hope of Restoration: Despite the message of judgment, Amos also speaks of the hope of restoration and renewal. He envisions a time when the people of Israel will turn back to God and when the land will be restored to its former prosperity.

Overall, the book of Amos is a powerful critique of the social, political, and religious conditions of ancient Israel. It challenges readers to examine their own lives and to work towards justice and righteousness, while also reminding them of the hope of restoration and renewal that comes through faithfulness to God.

The Judgment of God

Here are a few examples of verses from the book of Amos that speak about the judgment of God in the KJV translation:

- "Thus saith the Lord; For three transgressions of Israel, and for four, I will not turn away the punishment thereof; because they sold the righteous for silver, and the poor for a pair of shoes" (Amos 2:6).
- "Behold, the eyes of the Lord God are upon the sinful kingdom, and I will destroy it from off the face of the earth; saving that I will not utterly destroy the house of Jacob, saith the Lord" (Amos 9:8).
- "Therefore will I make thee go into captivity beyond Damascus, saith the Lord, whose name is The God of hosts" (Amos 5:27).
- "I hate, I despise your feast days, and I will not smell in your solemn assemblies" (Amos 5:21).

These verses emphasize the judgment of God upon Israel for their disobedience and unfaithfulness, including their mistreatment of the poor and their false worship.

Social Injustice

Here are a few examples of verses from the book of Amos that speak about social injustice in the KJV translation:

- "They sell the righteous for silver, and the poor for a pair of shoes" (Amos 2:6).
- "Hear this, O ye that swallow up the needy, even to make the poor of the

land to fail" (Amos 8:4).

- "Forasmuch therefore as your treading is upon the poor, and ye take from him burdens of wheat: ye have built houses of hewn stone, but ye shall not dwell in them; ye have planted pleasant vineyards, but ye shall not drink wine of them" (Amos 5:11).

These verses denounce the exploitation of the poor by the wealthy and powerful in Israel during Amos' time. The people were mistreating and taking advantage of those who were vulnerable, and Amos warns them of the consequences of their actions.

False Worship

Here are a few examples of verses from the book of Amos that speak about false worship in the KJV translation:

- "I hate, I despise your feast days, and I will not smell in your solemn assemblies. Though ye offer me burnt offerings and your meat offerings, I will not accept them: neither will I regard the peace offerings of your fat beasts" (Amos 5:21-22).
- "Take thou away from me the noise of thy songs; for I will not hear the melody of thy viols" (Amos 5:23).
- "But ye have borne the tabernacle of your Moloch and Chiun your images, the star of your god, which ye made to yourselves" (Amos 5:26).

These verses emphasize that the religious practices and rituals of Israel had become empty and meaningless. The people were engaging in false worship, offering sacrifices and playing music without true faith and obedience to God. Amos denounces these practices and calls for a return to true righteousness and justice.

The Sovereignty of God

Here are a few examples of verses from the book of Amos that speak about the sovereignty of God in the KJV translation:

- "The Lord will roar from Zion, and utter his voice from Jerusalem; and the habitations of the shepherds shall mourn, and the top of Carmel shall wither" (Amos 1:2).
- "He that formeth the mountains, and createth the wind, and declareth unto man what is his thought, that maketh the morning darkness, and treadeth upon the high places of the earth, The Lord, The God of hosts, is his name" (Amos 4:13).
- "For, lo, he that formeth the mountains, and createth the wind, and declareth unto man what is his thought, that maketh the morning darkness, and treadeth upon the high places of the earth, The Lord, The God of hosts, is his name" (Amos 5:8).

These verses emphasize the power and sovereignty of God, who is in control of all things and has the authority to judge and punish his people for their disobedience. Amos acknowledges God's power and calls upon the people to turn back to him in repentance and faithfulness.

The Hope of Restoration

Here are a few examples of verses from the book of Amos that speak about the hope of restoration in the KJV translation:

- "In that day will I raise up the tabernacle of David that is fallen, and close up the breaches thereof; and I will raise up his ruins, and I will build it as in the days of old" (Amos 9:11).
- "And I will bring again the captivity of my people of Israel, and they shall build the waste cities, and inhabit them; and they shall plant vineyards, and drink the wine thereof; they shall also make gardens, and eat the fruit

of them" (Amos 9:14).

- "And I will plant them upon their land, and they shall no more be pulled up out of their land which I have given them, saith the Lord thy God" (Amos 9:15).

These verses offer a message of hope and restoration for the people of Israel. Despite the judgment that is coming upon them for their disobedience, God promises to restore them and rebuild what has been destroyed. He promises to bring the people back to their land, to rebuild their cities and vineyards, and to establish them once again. Amos encourages the people to hold onto this hope and trust in God's promises.

6

Hosea - Minor Prophets(750-722 BC)

Hosea was a prophet who lived in the northern kingdom of Israel during the 8th century BCE, around the same time as Amos and Isaiah. He was the son of Beeri and his prophetic ministry spanned several decades, covering the reigns of multiple kings.

Hosea's personal life was intertwined with his prophetic message, as he was commanded by God to marry a woman named Gomer who was unfaithful to him. Their marriage was intended to serve as a metaphor for Israel's unfaithfulness to God. Hosea's three children were given symbolic names by God as well. The first child was a son named Jezreel, which means "God sows" and referred to the bloodshed that would come upon the house of Jehu. The second child was a daughter named Lo-Ruhamah, which means "not pitied" or "not loved", signifying that God would no longer have compassion on the house of Israel. The third child was a son named Lo-Ammi, which means "not my people", indicating that God would no longer acknowledge Israel as his people. However, in Hosea 2:1-3, God promises to restore Israel and change their name to "my people" once again

Hosea's message was primarily one of judgment and warning, as he spoke out against the idolatry, social injustice, and spiritual adultery that were rampant in Israel at the time. He also spoke of the coming judgment of God and the need for repentance and faithfulness.

Despite the strong message of judgment, Hosea also offered a message of hope and restoration, emphasizing God's love and mercy and the promise of a future restoration for the people of Israel.

Historical and Cultural Context

Hosea lived during a tumultuous time in the history of the northern kingdom of Israel. Following the reign of Jeroboam II, who brought a period of relative stability and prosperity to the kingdom, the nation was plunged into a period of political instability, social injustice, and spiritual decay.

During this time, the northern kingdom of Israel was plagued by a series of weak and ineffective kings who were unable to address the problems facing the nation. The people of Israel turned away from the worship of God and embraced the worship of false gods, including Baal and Asherah. This led to widespread idolatry and spiritual adultery, as the people of Israel abandoned their covenant relationship with God and turned to other gods and practices.

The political situation in Israel was also precarious, with the nation facing threats from neighboring nations such as Assyria and Aram. This led to a sense of insecurity and fear among the people, as they struggled to find security and stability in a rapidly changing world.

It was against this backdrop of political and social turmoil that Hosea prophesied, calling the people of Israel to repentance and faithfulness and warning them of the coming judgment of God. Hosea's message was a powerful indictment of the spiritual and moral decay that had taken hold in Israel, and it served as a powerful reminder of the need for repentance, faithfulness, and a return to God.

Importance

The book of Hosea is an important part of the Hebrew Bible. It offers a powerful message of God's love and mercy, even in the face of human rebellion and unfaithfulness.

Hosea's prophetic message speaks to the enduring problem of human sinfulness and rebellion against God, and offers a message of hope and restoration for those who turn back to God in repentance and faithfulness. The book also provides a vivid example of the prophetic tradition in ancient Israel, showing the important role that the prophets played in challenging the people of Israel to live up to their covenant relationship with God.

In addition to its theological significance, the book of Hosea is also notable for its literary style and structure. The book is written in a poetic form, with vivid imagery and powerful metaphors that convey the depth of God's love and the extent of human rebellion. The use of Hosea's own personal experience as a metaphor for God's relationship with Israel is also unique and powerful, emphasizing the personal and emotional nature of God's love and the depth of his desire for reconciliation with his people.

Overall, the book of Hosea offers a powerful message of God's love and mercy, as well as a challenge to turn away from sin and rebellion and to return to a faithful relationship with God. It is an important part of the prophetic tradition in ancient Israel and continues to speak to the enduring spiritual needs of people today.

Structure and Organization

The book of Hosea is structured around the prophet's life and message. The first three chapters describe Hosea's own personal life as a metaphor for God's relationship with Israel. Hosea is commanded by God to marry a woman named Gomer, who is unfaithful to him and has children with other men. Hosea's love for Gomer and his determination to reconcile with her, despite her unfaithfulness, serve as a powerful metaphor for God's love for Israel, and his determination to reconcile with his people, despite their unfaithfulness.

The rest of the book contains a series of oracles and messages from Hosea to the people of Israel. These oracles are organized around a series of themes, including judgment and punishment for Israel's sinfulness, the call to repentance and faithfulness, and the promise of restoration and reconciliation with God. The book also contains vivid descriptions of the idolatry and spiritual adultery of the people of Israel, as well as powerful images of God's love and mercy.

The overall structure of the book is a reflection of Hosea's prophetic message. It emphasizes the personal and emotional nature of God's relationship with Israel, and the depth of his love and desire for reconciliation with his people. It also serves as a powerful reminder of the need for repentance and faithfulness, and the promise of restoration and reconciliation with God for those who turn back to him.

Major themes

The book of Hosea contains several major themes that are important to understanding the prophet's message:

1. God's steadfast love and mercy: Hosea emphasizes God's enduring love and mercy, even in the face of Israel's unfaithfulness. Hosea describes God as a loving husband who seeks to reconcile with his unfaithful wife, Israel, and who continues to show compassion and mercy towards his people.
2. Israel's unfaithfulness and sinfulness: Hosea speaks out against the spiritual adultery and idolatry of the people of Israel, who have turned away from God and pursued false gods and idols.
3. Judgment and punishment: Hosea warns that Israel's unfaithfulness will lead to judgment and punishment from God. He describes the coming destruction of Israel and the Assyrian invasion as a result of their disobedience.
4. The call to repentance and faithfulness: Despite the judgment and punishment that Israel faces, Hosea emphasizes the need for repentance and faithfulness. He calls on the people of Israel to turn away from their idols and false gods, and to return to God in repentance and faithfulness.
5. Restoration and reconciliation: Hosea also speaks of the promise of restoration and reconciliation with God for those who turn back to him in repentance and faithfulness. He describes a future time when God will restore Israel and renew their covenant relationship with him.

Overall, the book of Hosea offers a powerful message of God's love and mercy, as well as a challenge to turn away from sin and rebellion and to return to a faithful relationship with God. It is a powerful call to repentance and renewal, and a reminder of the enduring nature of God's love for his people.

God's steadfast love and mercy

Here are some verses from the book of Hosea in the King James Version (KJV) that speak of God's steadfast love and mercy:

1. "I will betroth thee unto me for ever; yea, I will betroth thee unto me in righteousness, and in judgment, and in lovingkindness, and in mercies." - Hosea 2:19
2. "I drew them with cords of a man, with bands of love: and I was to them as they that take off the yoke on their jaws, and I laid meat unto them." - Hosea 11:4
3. "How shall I give thee up, Ephraim? how shall I deliver thee, Israel? how shall I make thee as Admah? how shall I set thee as Zeboim? mine heart is turned within me, my repentings are kindled together." - Hosea 11:8
4. "I will heal their backsliding, I will love them freely: for mine anger is turned away from him." - Hosea 14:4
5. "Who is wise, and he shall understand these things? prudent, and he shall know them? for the ways of the LORD are right, and the just shall walk in them: but the transgressors shall fall therein." - Hosea 14:9

These verses illustrate the deep love and compassion that God has for his people, even in the face of their unfaithfulness and rebellion. Despite their sinfulness, God continues to extend his mercy and grace towards them, offering the promise of forgiveness and reconciliation for those who turn back to him in repentance and faith.

Israel's unfaithfulness and sinfulness

Here are some verses from the book of Hosea in the King James Version (KJV) that speak of Israel's unfaithfulness and sinfulness:

1. "The beginning of the word of the LORD by Hosea. And the LORD said to Hosea, Go, take unto thee a wife of whoredoms and children of whoredoms: for the land hath committed great whoredom, departing from the LORD." - Hosea 1:2
2. "My people are destroyed for lack of knowledge: because thou hast rejected knowledge, I will also reject thee, that thou shalt be no priest to me: seeing thou hast forgotten the law of thy God, I will also forget thy children." - Hosea 4:6
3. "For Israel slideth back as a backsliding heifer: now the LORD will feed them as a lamb in a large place." - Hosea 4:16
4. "They have deeply corrupted themselves, as in the days of Gibeah: therefore he will remember their iniquity, he will visit their sins." - Hosea 9:9
5. "Ephraim is joined to idols: let him alone." - Hosea 4:17

These verses illustrate the unfaithfulness and sinfulness of Israel during Hosea's time, with the people turning away from God and engaging in idolatry, immorality, and other forms of wickedness. Despite God's repeated warnings and calls for repentance, the people persist in their disobedience, leading to judgment and punishment. However, even in the midst of this judgment, God's love and mercy continue to shine through, offering the hope of redemption and restoration for those who turn back to him in humility and faith.

Judgment and punishment

Here are some verses from the book of Hosea in the King James Version (KJV) that speak of God's judgment and punishment:

1. "Therefore will I be unto them as a lion: as a leopard by the way will I observe them: I will meet them as a bear that is bereaved of her whelps, and will rend the caul of their heart, and there will I devour them like a lion: the wild beast shall tear them." - Hosea 13:7-8
2. "I will go and return to my place, till they acknowledge their offence, and seek my face: in their affliction they will seek me early." - Hosea 5:15
3. "They have sown the wind, and they shall reap the whirlwind: it hath no stalk: the bud shall yield no meal: if so be it yield, the strangers shall swallow it up." - Hosea 8:7
4. "Ephraim is smitten, their root is dried up, they shall bear no fruit: yea, though they bring forth, yet will I slay even the beloved fruit of their womb." - Hosea 9:16
5. "I will not execute the fierceness of mine anger, I will not return to destroy Ephraim: for I am God, and not man; the Holy One in the midst of thee: and I will not enter into the city." - Hosea 11:9

These verses illustrate the judgment and punishment that God pronounces upon Israel for their sins and unfaithfulness. The imagery is vivid and powerful, depicting God as a fierce lion or wild beast, ready to tear and devour those who have turned away from him. The consequences of Israel's actions are severe, with the people reaping the whirlwind of their own wickedness and suffering the loss of their children and fruitfulness. Despite this, however, there is also a note of hope and mercy, with God promising to withhold his anger and not completely destroy his people, even in the midst of their disobedience.

The call to repentance and faithfulness

Here are some verses from the book of Hosea in the King James Version (KJV) that call for repentance and faithfulness:

1. "Sow to yourselves in righteousness, reap in mercy; break up your fallow ground: for it is time to seek the Lord, till he come and rain righteousness upon you." - Hosea 10:12
2. "Take with you words, and turn to the Lord: say unto him, Take away all iniquity, and receive us graciously: so will we render the calves of our lips." - Hosea 14:2
3. "Come, and let us return unto the Lord: for he hath torn, and he will heal us; he hath smitten, and he will bind us up." - Hosea 6:1
4. "O Israel, return unto the Lord thy God; for thou hast fallen by thine iniquity." - Hosea 14:1
5. "Therefore also now, saith the Lord, turn ye even to me with all your heart, and with fasting, and with weeping, and with mourning:" - Hosea 2:12

These verses call for Israel to repent and turn back to God, acknowledging their sins and seeking his forgiveness and mercy. The language is often poetic and evocative, emphasizing the urgency of the call and the need for a deep and genuine change of heart. The imagery of sowing and reaping righteousness, breaking up fallow ground, and returning to the Lord all emphasize the idea of turning away from sin and back towards God's ways. Despite the severity of God's judgment and the weight of Israel's sins, there is always the possibility of forgiveness and redemption for those who are willing to seek it.

Restoration and reconciliation

Here are some verses from the book of Hosea in the King James Version (KJV) that speak about restoration and reconciliation:

1. "I will heal their backsliding, I will love them freely: for mine anger is turned away from him." - Hosea 14:4
2. "Then shall we know, if we follow on to know the Lord: his going forth is prepared as the morning; and he shall come unto us as the rain, as the latter and former rain unto the earth." - Hosea 6:3
3. "I will be as the dew unto Israel: he shall grow as the lily, and cast forth his roots as Lebanon." - Hosea 14:5
4. "And I will betroth thee unto me for ever; yea, I will betroth thee unto me in righteousness, and in judgment, and in lovingkindness, and in mercies." - Hosea 2:19
5. "And I will sow her unto me in the earth; and I will have mercy upon her that had not obtained mercy; and I will say to them which were not my people, Thou art my people; and they shall say, Thou art my God." - Hosea 2:23

These verses speak of God's willingness to forgive and restore Israel despite their unfaithfulness and sinfulness. They emphasize the depth of God's love and mercy, and the hope of reconciliation and healing that comes through turning back to him. The language of betrothal and sowing emphasizes the idea of a deep and lasting relationship between God and his people, rooted in righteousness, judgment, lovingkindness, and mercy. The imagery of growth and renewal emphasizes the idea of a new beginning, a fresh start, and a bright future for those who turn to God with repentance and faith.

7

Isaiah - Major Prophet (740-700 BC)

The name Isaiah means "Yahweh is salvation" or "salvation of the Lord" in Hebrew. The name is derived from the words "yasha", meaning "to save", and "Yah", a shortened form of the name of God in the Hebrew Bible, Yahweh. The name reflects the central message of Isaiah's prophetic ministry, which was to call the people of Israel to repentance and faithfulness, and to proclaim the salvation that God offers through His grace and mercy.

Isaiah was a prophet in the Old Testament who lived in the 8th century BC, during the reigns of several kings of Judah. He was likely born into a prominent family and had a good education, as evidenced by his literary style and knowledge of political events.

Isaiah began his prophetic ministry around 740 BC, during the reign of King Uzziah. He continued to prophesy throughout the reigns of Jotham, Ahaz, and Hezekiah, and may have lived into the reign of King Manasseh. Isaiah's ministry took place during a time of great political and social turmoil in Israel and Judah, as the two kingdoms faced threats from neighboring nations, including Assyria and Babylon.

Isaiah's prophetic message emphasized the sovereignty and power of God, the sinfulness and unfaithfulness of the people of Israel and Judah, and the coming of the Messiah. He also warned of impending judgment and exile, but also promised eventual restoration and salvation.

Isaiah's prophecies were often delivered through poetic language and symbolic imagery, making his message both powerful and memorable. Many of his prophecies have been fulfilled, such as the fall of Babylon and the coming of the Messiah, and his writings continue to be studied and revered by believers today.

Historical Cultural Context

Isaiah lived during a significant period of Israel's history, which was marked by political, social, and religious changes. He prophesied during the reigns of several kings of Judah, a time that is commonly referred to as the Divided Monarchy. This period began after the death of King Solomon and the division of the kingdom of Israel into two separate kingdoms - the northern kingdom of Israel and the southern kingdom of Judah.

During Isaiah's time, the northern kingdom of Israel was in decline and eventually fell to the Assyrian empire in 722 BC. The southern kingdom of Judah faced threats from various neighboring nations, including Assyria and Babylon, and was eventually conquered by the Babylonians in 586 BC. These events had a significant impact on the people of Judah and helped shape Isaiah's message of warning and hope.

The Assyrians, who were one of the major world powers at the time, posed a significant threat to the kingdoms of Israel and Judah. They were known for their brutal military campaigns and were responsible for the destruction of the northern kingdom of Israel. Isaiah warned the people of Judah about the coming Assyrian invasion and called for repentance and faithfulness to God.

The Babylonians were another major world power during Isaiah's time, and they eventually conquered Judah and destroyed the temple in Jerusalem. This event marked the beginning of the Babylonian exile, which lasted for several decades. Isaiah prophesied about the coming of the Babylonians and the eventual restoration of Israel, which would be led by a figure known as the Messiah.

In addition to the political and military events of the time, Isaiah also spoke out against social injustice, idolatry, and false prophets. He emphasized the importance of worshiping the one true God and living in obedience to his commands.

Overall, the historical and cultural context in which Isaiah lived was characterized by political instability, social upheaval, and religious turmoil. His message of warning, judgment, and hope spoke directly to the challenges and concerns of the people of his time, and continues to inspire and challenge believers today.

Importance

The book of Isaiah is considered one of the most important and influential books in the Bible. Here are some of the reasons why:

1. Prophecies of the coming Messiah: The book of Isaiah contains numerous prophecies about the coming of the Messiah, who would save God's people from sin and oppression. These prophecies are some of the most well-known and significant passages in the Bible and have been fulfilled in the person of Jesus Christ.
2. Themes of judgment and restoration: Isaiah's message emphasized the importance of faithfulness and obedience to God, warning of impending judgment for sin and rebellion. However, he also promised eventual restoration and salvation for those who would repent and turn back to God.
3. Symbolic language and imagery: Isaiah's prophetic message is often delivered through poetic language and symbolic imagery, making his message both powerful and memorable.
4. Theological and doctrinal significance: The book of Isaiah contains important teachings about God's nature, the role of the Messiah, and the relationship between God and his people. These teachings have been foundational to Christian theology and doctrine.
5. Historical context: The book of Isaiah provides important historical context for understanding the political and social events of the time, as well as the religious practices and beliefs of the people of Israel and Judah.

Overall, the book of Isaiah has been valued and studied by believers throughout history for its powerful message of judgment and restoration, its prophecies of the coming Messiah, and its theological and historical significance.

Structure and Organization

The book of Isaiah is divided into two main parts: First Isaiah (chapters 1-39) and Second Isaiah (chapters 40-66). Some Scholars believe that these two sections were written by different authors at different times, and that they reflect different historical and cultural contexts.

First Isaiah, which is also known as Proto-Isaiah, is primarily concerned with the Assyrian threat to Judah and the need for repentance and faithfulness to God. The section begins with a message of judgment and condemnation for the sins of Judah, but also offers hope for restoration and salvation. The first part of the book contains many memorable passages and prophecies, including the vision of the Lord in Isaiah 6 and the prophecy of the virgin birth in Isaiah 7.

Second Isaiah, which is also known as Deutero-Isaiah, was written during the Babylonian exile, after the fall of Judah and the destruction of the temple in Jerusalem. This section is characterized by a message of comfort and hope for the exiled Israelites, with a focus on the coming of the Messiah and the eventual restoration of Israel. Some of the most well-known passages in the book of Isaiah are found in Second Isaiah, including the prophecy of the suffering servant in Isaiah 53 and the declaration of God's sovereignty in Isaiah 40.

In addition to these two main sections, the book of Isaiah also contains several interludes and appendices, including the prophecies against Babylon (Isaiah 13-14) and the hymn of praise in Isaiah 12.

Overall, the book of Isaiah is a rich and complex work, containing a variety of literary genres and styles. The structure and organization of the book reflect the historical and cultural context in which it was written, as well as the themes and messages that are developed throughout the book.

Major Themes

The book of Isaiah contains several major themes that are developed throughout the book. Here are some of the main themes:

1. Judgment and salvation: One of the main themes of Isaiah is the importance of faithfulness and obedience to God. The book contains many warnings of judgment and condemnation for the sins of Judah and Israel, but also offers hope for restoration and salvation.
2. The sovereignty and power of God: Isaiah emphasizes the power and sovereignty of God, who is the creator and ruler of the universe. This theme is developed through the use of poetic language and imagery, such as the vision of the Lord in Isaiah 6.
3. Israel's unfaithfulness and disobedience: Isaiah criticizes the people of Israel and Judah for their unfaithfulness and disobedience to God. He condemns their idolatry, social injustice, and false worship, and calls for repentance and a return to the ways of God.
4. The coming of the Messiah: Isaiah contains numerous prophecies of the coming of the Messiah, who would save God's people from sin and oppression. These prophecies are some of the most well-known and significant passages in the Bible and have been fulfilled in the person of Jesus Christ.
5. The restoration of Israel: Isaiah prophesies about the eventual restoration of Israel, which would be led by a figure known as the Messiah. This theme is developed in Second Isaiah, which was written during the Babylonian exile and emphasizes the hope of restoration for the exiled Israelites.
6. The universal scope of God's plan: Isaiah emphasizes that God's plan extends beyond Israel and Judah, and that all nations will eventually come to worship him. This theme is developed through prophecies about the nations and the inclusion of non-Israelite figures, such as Cyrus the Persian, in the book.

Overall, these themes provide a framework for understanding the message of Isaiah and offer insights into the nature and character of God.

Judgment and salvation

These verses from Isaiah in KJV relate to the theme of judgment and salvation:

1. Isaiah 1:16-18 - "Wash you, make you clean; put away the evil of your doings from before mine eyes; cease to do evil; Learn to do well; seek judgment, relieve the oppressed, judge the fatherless, plead for the widow. Come now, and let us reason together, saith the Lord: though your sins be as scarlet, they shall be as white as snow; though they be red like crimson, they shall be as wool."
2. Isaiah 5:20 - "Woe unto them that call evil good, and good evil; that put darkness for light, and light for darkness; that put bitter for sweet, and sweet for bitter!"
3. Isaiah 9:6-7 - "For unto us a child is born, unto us a son is given: and the government shall be upon his shoulder: and his name shall be called Wonderful, Counsellor, The mighty God, The everlasting Father, The Prince of Peace. Of the increase of his government and peace there shall be no end, upon the throne of David, and upon his kingdom, to order it, and to establish it with judgment and with justice from henceforth even for ever. The zeal of the Lord of hosts will perform this."
4. Isaiah 53:5-6 - "But he was wounded for our transgressions, he was bruised for our iniquities: the chastisement of our peace was upon him; and with his stripes we are healed. All we like sheep have gone astray; we have turned every one to his own way; and the Lord hath laid on him the iniquity of us all."
5. Isaiah 55:6-7 - "Seek ye the Lord while he may be found, call ye upon him while he is near: Let the wicked forsake his way, and the unrighteous man his thoughts: and let him return unto the Lord, and he will have mercy upon him; and to our God, for he will abundantly pardon."

These verses in the King James Version demonstrate the same tension between God's judgment and salvation, calling for repentance and obedience while also offering the hope of forgiveness and restoration.

The sovereignty and power of God

Here are some verses from Isaiah in the King James Version that emphasize the sovereignty and power of God:

1. Isaiah 6:1-3 - "In the year that king Uzziah died I saw also the Lord sitting upon a throne, high and lifted up, and his train filled the temple. Above it stood the seraphims: each one had six wings; with twain he covered his face, and with twain he covered his feet, and with twain he did fly. And one cried unto another, and said, Holy, holy, holy, is the Lord of hosts: the whole earth is full of his glory."
2. Isaiah 40:28 - "Hast thou not known? hast thou not heard, that the everlasting God, the Lord, the Creator of the ends of the earth, fainteth not, neither is weary? there is no searching of his understanding."
3. Isaiah 45:5-7 - "I am the Lord, and there is none else, there is no God beside me: I girded thee, though thou hast not known me: That they may know from the rising of the sun, and from the west, that there is none beside me. I am the Lord, and there is none else. I form the light, and create darkness: I make peace, and create evil: I the Lord do all these things."
4. Isaiah 46:9-10 - "Remember the former things of old: for I am God, and there is none else; I am God, and there is none like me, Declaring the end from the beginning, and from ancient times the things that are not yet done, saying, My counsel shall stand, and I will do all my pleasure."
5. Isaiah 48:17 - "Thus saith the Lord, thy Redeemer, the Holy One of Israel; I am the Lord thy God which teacheth thee to profit, which leadeth thee by the way that thou shouldest go."

These verses emphasize the power, sovereignty, and wisdom of God, and highlight his unique position as the creator and ruler of the universe. They remind us of the greatness and majesty of God, and inspire us to worship and trust in him.

Israel's unfaithfulness and disobedience

Here are some verses from Isaiah in the King James Version that relate to Israel's unfaithfulness and disobedience:

1. Isaiah 1:2-4 - "Hear, O heavens, and give ear, O earth: for the Lord hath spoken, I have nourished and brought up children, and they have rebelled against me. The ox knoweth his owner, and the ass his master's crib: but Israel doth not know, my people doth not consider. Ah sinful nation, a people laden with iniquity, a seed of evildoers, children that are corrupters: they have forsaken the Lord, they have provoked the Holy One of Israel unto anger, they are gone away backward."
2. Isaiah 5:24-25 - "Therefore as the fire devoureth the stubble, and the flame consumeth the chaff, so their root shall be as rottenness, and their blossom shall go up as dust: because they have cast away the law of the Lord of hosts, and despised the word of the Holy One of Israel. Therefore is the anger of the Lord kindled against his people, and he hath stretched forth his hand against them, and hath smitten them: and the hills did tremble, and their carcases were torn in the midst of the streets. For all this his anger is not turned away, but his hand is stretched out still."
3. Isaiah 29:13 - "Wherefore the Lord said, Forasmuch as this people draw near me with their mouth, and with their lips do honour me, but have removed their heart far from me, and their fear toward me is taught by the precept of men."
4. Isaiah 59:2 - "But your iniquities have separated between you and your God, and your sins have hid his face from you, that he will not hear."
5. Isaiah 65:2-3 - "I have spread out my hands all the day unto a rebellious people, which walketh in a way that was not good, after their own thoughts; A people that provoketh me to anger continually to my face;

that sacrificeth in gardens, and burneth incense upon altars of brick."

These verses highlight the sinfulness and rebellion of Israel, and emphasize the consequences of their disobedience. They serve as a warning to us to avoid the same pitfalls of disobedience and unfaithfulness, and to seek repentance and obedience to God.

The coming of the Messiah

Here are some verses from Isaiah in the King James Version that prophesy about the coming of the Messiah:

1. Isaiah 7:14 - "Therefore the Lord himself shall give you a sign; Behold, a virgin shall conceive, and bear a son, and shall call his name Immanuel."
2. Isaiah 9:6 - "For unto us a child is born, unto us a son is given: and the government shall be upon his shoulder: and his name shall be called Wonderful, Counsellor, The mighty God, The everlasting Father, The Prince of Peace."
3. Isaiah 11:1-2 - "And there shall come forth a rod out of the stem of Jesse, and a Branch shall grow out of his roots: And the spirit of the Lord shall rest upon him, the spirit of wisdom and understanding, the spirit of counsel and might, the spirit of knowledge and of the fear of the Lord."
4. Isaiah 42:1-4 - "Behold my servant, whom I uphold; mine elect, in whom my soul delighteth; I have put my spirit upon him: he shall bring forth judgment to the Gentiles. He shall not cry, nor lift up, nor cause his voice to be heard in the street. A bruised reed shall he not break, and the smoking flax shall he not quench: he shall bring forth judgment unto truth. He shall not fail nor be discouraged, till he have set judgment in the earth: and the isles shall wait for his law."
5. Isaiah 53:3-5 - "He is despised and rejected of men; a man of sorrows, and acquainted with grief: and we hid as it were our faces from him; he was despised, and we esteemed him not. Surely he hath borne our griefs, and carried our sorrows: yet we did esteem him stricken, smitten of God,

and afflicted. But he was wounded for our transgressions, he was bruised for our iniquities: the chastisement of our peace was upon him; and with his stripes we are healed."

These verses prophesy about the coming of a savior, who would be born of a virgin, be anointed by God, and bring justice and righteousness to the earth. They also predict that he would suffer and die for the sins of humanity. These prophecies have been fulfilled in the person of Jesus Christ.

The restoration of Israel

Here are some verses from Isaiah in the King James Version that relate to the restoration of Israel:

1. Isaiah 10:20-22 - "And it shall come to pass in that day, that the remnant of Israel, and such as are escaped of the house of Jacob, shall no more again stay upon him that smote them; but shall stay upon the Lord, the Holy One of Israel, in truth. The remnant shall return, even the remnant of Jacob, unto the mighty God. For though thy people Israel be as the sand of the sea, yet a remnant of them shall return: the consumption decreed shall overflow with righteousness."
2. Isaiah 11:11-12 - "And it shall come to pass in that day, that the Lord shall set his hand again the second time to recover the remnant of his people, which shall be left, from Assyria, and from Egypt, and from Pathros, and from Cush, and from Elam, and from Shinar, and from Hamath, and from the islands of the sea. And he shall set up an ensign for the nations, and shall assemble the outcasts of Israel, and gather together the dispersed of Judah from the four corners of the earth."
3. Isaiah 44:21-23 - "Remember these, O Jacob and Israel; for thou art my servant: I have formed thee; thou art my servant: O Israel, thou shalt not be forgotten of me. I have blotted out, as a thick cloud, thy transgressions, and, as a cloud, thy sins: return unto me; for I have redeemed thee. Sing, O ye heavens; for the Lord hath done it: shout, ye

lower parts of the earth: break forth into singing, ye mountains, O forest, and every tree therein: for the Lord hath redeemed Jacob, and glorified himself in Israel."

4. Isaiah 49:8-9 - "Thus saith the Lord, In an acceptable time have I heard thee, and in a day of salvation have I helped thee: and I will preserve thee, and give thee for a covenant of the people, to establish the earth, to cause to inherit the desolate heritages; That thou mayest say to the prisoners, Go forth; to them that are in darkness, Shew yourselves. They shall feed in the ways, and their pastures shall be in all high places."
5. Isaiah 62:1-2 - "For Zion's sake will I not hold my peace, and for Jerusalem's sake I will not rest, until the righteousness thereof go forth as brightness, and the salvation thereof as a lamp that burneth. And the Gentiles shall see thy righteousness, and all kings thy glory: and thou shalt be called by a new name, which the mouth of the Lord shall name."

These verses prophesy about the restoration of Israel and the regathering of the 12 tribes to their land. They describe the Lord's faithfulness to his covenant with Israel and his promise to redeem them from their sins and restore them to their former glory.

Universal scope of God's plan

Here are some verses from the book of Isaiah in the KJV Bible that emphasize the universal scope of God's plan:

1. Isaiah 2:2 - "And it shall come to pass in the last days, that the mountain of the Lord's house shall be established in the top of the mountains, and shall be exalted above the hills; and all nations shall flow unto it."
2. Isaiah 11:10 - "And in that day there shall be a root of Jesse, which shall stand for an ensign of the people; to it shall the Gentiles seek: and his rest shall be glorious."
3. Isaiah 19:23-25 - "In that day shall there be a highway out of Egypt to Assyria, and the Assyrian shall come into Egypt, and the Egyptian into

Assyria, and the Egyptians shall serve with the Assyrians. In that day shall Israel be the third with Egypt and with Assyria, even a blessing in the midst of the land: Whom the Lord of hosts shall bless, saying, Blessed be Egypt my people, and Assyria the work of my hands, and Israel mine inheritance."

4. Isaiah 25:6-8 - "And in this mountain shall the Lord of hosts make unto all people a feast of fat things, a feast of wines on the lees, of fat things full of marrow, of wines on the lees well refined. And he will destroy in this mountain the face of the covering cast over all people, and the vail that is spread over all nations. He will swallow up death in victory; and the Lord God will wipe away tears from off all faces; and the rebuke of his people shall he take away from off all the earth: for the Lord hath spoken it."
5. Isaiah 42:6 - "I the Lord have called thee in righteousness, and will hold thine hand, and will keep thee, and give thee for a covenant of the people, for a light of the Gentiles;"
6. Isaiah 49:6 - "And he said, It is a light thing that thou shouldest be my servant to raise up the tribes of Jacob, and to restore the preserved of Israel: I will also give thee for a light to the Gentiles, that thou mayest be my salvation unto the end of the earth."

These verses demonstrate that God's plan of salvation is not limited to one nation or people, but is intended for all people and all nations.

8

Micah - Minor Prophet (735-700 BC)

Micah was a prophet who lived in the 8th century BC in Judah, during the reigns of Jotham, Ahaz, and Hezekiah. He was a contemporary of Isaiah and Hosea, and his prophetic ministry likely spanned several decades. Micah was from the town of Moresheth in Judah, and his name means "Who is like Yahweh?"

Micah was known for his powerful preaching against social and religious injustice in Judah. He spoke out against the oppression of the poor, the abuse of power by the ruling class, and the syncretistic worship practices that had crept into the nation. He also warned of impending judgment and exile, but held out hope for restoration and renewal through repentance and faithfulness to God.

Micah's prophetic message was deeply rooted in the covenantal relationship between God and his people. He reminded the people of their obligations to love God and to love their neighbors, and he challenged them to live out these principles in their daily lives. Micah's message of social justice and the call to a genuine faith in God remains relevant and inspiring to this day.

Historical and Cultural Context

The prophet Micah lived during a time of political and social upheaval in the southern kingdom of Judah. He prophesied during the reigns of three kings: Jotham, Ahaz, and Hezekiah, between approximately 735 and 700 BCE.

During this period, the northern kingdom of Israel had already been destroyed by the Assyrians, and Judah was under threat from the rising power of the Assyrian empire. The Assyrians were known for their brutal conquests and their practice of deporting conquered peoples to other lands, which led to the displacement of many Israelites and Judahites.

In addition to these external pressures, there were also internal problems within Judah, including social injustice, corruption, and religious apostasy. Micah spoke out against these issues and called for repentance, social reform, and a return to faithfulness to God.

The cultural context in which Micah lived was one of political and religious syncretism, as Judah was influenced by the neighboring nations of Assyria and Babylon. Micah's prophetic message was a call to reject these foreign gods and idols and to worship the one true God of Israel.

Importance

The book of Micah is considered one of the major prophetic books of the Old Testament and is of great importance in the Bible for several reasons.

Firstly, Micah's prophetic message is a powerful reminder of God's justice and righteousness. Micah denounces social injustice and oppression, warning of God's judgment on those who exploit the poor and vulnerable. His message also emphasizes the importance of personal morality and ethical behavior, as well as the need for repentance and spiritual renewal.

Secondly, Micah's prophecies about the coming of the Messiah are significant in their detail and specificity. Micah predicts that the Messiah will be born in Bethlehem and will rule over Israel as a shepherd-king, a prophecy that is later fulfilled in the person of Jesus Christ.

Finally, Micah's message of hope and restoration is a central theme throughout the book. Despite the judgment that he predicts, Micah also offers a message of hope for the future, promising that God will ultimately restore his people and establish a new era of peace and prosperity.

Overall, the book of Micah provides a powerful and enduring message of God's justice, mercy, and faithfulness, and its themes continue to resonate with readers today.

Structure and organization

The book of Micah is divided into seven chapters, each containing a distinct message or theme.

Chapter 1 begins with a call to attention and judgment against Israel and Judah, as well as against their neighboring nations.

Chapter 2 focuses on social injustice and the oppression of the poor, specifically by the wealthy and powerful in society.

Chapter 3 is a denunciation of the corrupt leaders and false prophets who have led the people astray and who will face God's judgment.

Chapter 4 is a message of hope and restoration, predicting a time of peace and prosperity when nations will come to Jerusalem to learn from God.

Chapter 5 contains the well-known prophecy of the birthplace of the Messiah in Bethlehem, as well as the promise of God's protection and deliverance for his people.

Chapter 6 is a message of rebuke and repentance, calling the people to remember their covenant with God and to turn away from their sins.

Finally, Chapter 7 is a prayer of confession and plea for forgiveness, expressing the hope and trust that God will ultimately restore his people and bring about justice and righteousness.

Overall, the book of Micah has a clear structure and organization, with each chapter building upon the themes and messages of the previous ones to convey a powerful and cohesive prophetic message.

Major themes

1. Judgment and punishment for sin: Micah speaks out against the sins of Israel and Judah, and warns of the impending judgment that will come as a result.
2. The sovereignty of God: Micah emphasizes that God is in control of all things, including the actions of nations and individuals.
3. The hope of restoration: Despite the judgment that is to come, Micah offers a message of hope, promising that God will restore his people and establish his kingdom.
4. Social justice: Micah condemns the social injustices of his day, such as the exploitation of the poor and the abuse of power by those in authority.
5. True worship: Micah calls for a return to genuine worship of God, emphasizing that outward religious observances are meaningless without a heart that is truly devoted to God.

Judgment and punishment for sin

here are some verses from the book of Micah in the King James Version that speak about judgment and punishment for sin:

- Micah 1:5: "For the transgression of Jacob is all this, and for the sins of the house of Israel. What is the transgression of Jacob? is it not Samaria? and what are the high places of Judah? are they not Jerusalem?"
- Micah 2:1: "Woe to them that devise iniquity, and work evil upon their beds! when the morning is light, they practise it, because it is in the power of their hand."
- Micah 3:4: "Then shall they cry unto the Lord, but he will not hear them: he will even hide his face from them at that time, as they have behaved themselves ill in their doings."
- Micah 6:13-14: "Therefore also will I make thee sick in smiting thee, in making thee desolate because of thy sins. Thou shalt eat, but not be satisfied; and thy casting down shall be in the midst of thee; and thou

shalt take hold, but shalt not deliver; and that which thou deliverest will I give up to the sword."

- Micah 7:9: "I will bear the indignation of the Lord, because I have sinned against him, until he plead my cause, and execute judgment for me: he will bring me forth to the light, and I shall behold his righteousness."

These verses show that Micah prophesied about the judgment and punishment that God would bring upon his people for their sins and transgressions.

The sovereignty of God

Here are some verses in the book of Micah that speak of the sovereignty of God:

1. Micah 1:3 - "For, behold, the LORD cometh forth out of his place, and will come down, and tread upon the high places of the earth."
2. Micah 1:4 - "And the mountains shall be molten under him, and the valleys shall be cleft, as wax before the fire, and as the waters that are poured down a steep place."
3. Micah 4:13 - "Arise and thresh, O daughter of Zion: for I will make thine horn iron, and I will make thy hoofs brass: and thou shalt beat in pieces many people: and I will consecrate their gain unto the LORD, and their substance unto the Lord of the whole earth."
4. Micah 5:2 - "But thou, Bethlehem Ephratah, though thou be little among the thousands of Judah, yet out of thee shall he come forth unto me that is to be ruler in Israel; whose goings forth have been from of old, from everlasting."
5. Micah 5:4 - "And he shall stand and feed in the strength of the LORD, in the majesty of the name of the LORD his God; and they shall abide: for now shall he be great unto the ends of the earth."

These verses speak of the power and authority of God, who rules over all things and has the ability to bring judgment and destruction upon the earth.

They also speak of his sovereignty in choosing and anointing leaders, as seen in the reference to Bethlehem and the coming ruler of Israel. Ultimately, these verses remind us that God is in control and his plans and purposes will ultimately prevail.

The hope of restoration

Here are some verses in the book of Micah that speak about the hope of restoration:

1. "But in the last days it shall come to pass, that the mountain of the house of the Lord shall be established in the top of the mountains, and it shall be exalted above the hills; and people shall flow unto it." - Micah 4:1
2. "In that day, saith the Lord, will I assemble her that halteth, and I will gather her that is driven out, and her that I have afflicted;" - Micah 4:6
3. "And I will execute vengeance in anger and fury upon the heathen, such as they have not heard." - Micah 5:15
4. "He will turn again, he will have compassion upon us; he will subdue our iniquities; and thou wilt cast all their sins into the depths of the sea." - Micah 7:19

These verses speak of a future time when the Lord will restore his people and establish his kingdom. They offer hope and assurance that even in the midst of judgment and punishment, God is a merciful and loving God who desires to restore and redeem his people.

Social justice

Here are some verses from the book of Micah that touch on the theme of social justice:

1. Micah 2:1-2 - "Woe to those who plan iniquity, to those who plot evil on their beds! At morning's light they carry it out because it is in their power

to do it. They covet fields and seize them, and houses, and take them. They defraud people of their homes, they rob them of their inheritance."

2. Micah 3:1-3 - "Then I said, 'Listen, you leaders of Jacob, you rulers of Israel. Should you not embrace justice, you who hate good and love evil; who tear the skin from my people and the flesh from their bones; who eat my people's flesh, strip off their skin and break their bones in pieces; who chop them up like meat for the pan, like flesh for the pot?'"
3. Micah 6:8 - "He has shown you, O mortal, what is good. And what does the Lord require of you? To act justly and to love mercy and to walk humbly with your God."
4. Micah 6:11-12 - "Shall I acquit someone with dishonest scales, with a bag of false weights? Your rich people are violent; your inhabitants are liars and their tongues speak deceitfully."
5. Micah 7:2-3 - "The faithful have been swept from the land; not one upright person remains. Everyone lies in wait to shed blood; they hunt each other with nets. Both hands are skilled in doing evil; the ruler demands gifts, the judge accepts bribes, the powerful dictate what they desire—they all conspire together."

These verses speak to the injustice and corruption present in Micah's society, and his call for social justice and righteousness. They emphasize the importance of acting justly and loving mercy, and warn against the consequences of dishonesty and oppression.

True worship

Here are some verses from Micah in the King James Version that discuss true worship:

- Micah 6:6-8: "Wherewith shall I come before the Lord, and bow myself before the high God? shall I come before him with burnt offerings, with calves of a year old? Will the Lord be pleased with thousands of rams, or with ten thousands of rivers of oil? shall I give my firstborn for my transgression, the fruit of my body for the sin of my soul? He hath shewed thee, O man, what is good; and what doth the Lord require of thee, but to do justly, and to love mercy, and to walk humbly with thy God?"

In these verses, Micah is questioning what the proper way to worship God is. He asks if God would be pleased with sacrifices or offerings, but then goes on to say that what God truly requires is for people to act justly, love mercy, and walk humbly with Him.

- Micah 4:1-2: "But in the last days it shall come to pass, that the mountain of the house of the Lord shall be established in the top of the mountains, and it shall be exalted above the hills; and people shall flow unto it. And many nations shall come, and say, Come, and let us go up to the mountain of the Lord, and to the house of the God of Jacob; and he will teach us of his ways, and we will walk in his paths: for the law shall go forth of Zion, and the word of the Lord from Jerusalem."

In these verses, Micah speaks of a future time when people from many nations will come to worship God in Jerusalem. This emphasizes the universality of true worship and how it is not limited to any one group of people.

- Micah 5:4: "And he shall stand and feed in the strength of the Lord, in the majesty of the name of the Lord his God; and they shall abide: for now shall he be great unto the ends of the earth."

This verse speaks of a future ruler who will come from Bethlehem and will be great throughout the entire world. This emphasizes the importance of worshipping the true God, who is not limited by any geographic boundaries or cultural barriers.

9

Nahum - Minor Prophet (663-612 BC)

The name Nahum means "comfort" or "consolation" in Hebrew.

The prophet Nahum lived during the 7th century BC in a time when the Assyrian Empire was at the height of its power. The Assyrians had conquered much of the ancient Near East, including the northern kingdom of Israel, and were known for their cruelty and brutality in war. It was a time of great instability and fear, with many smaller kingdoms and city-states struggling to maintain their independence and avoid becoming victims of the Assyrian war machine.

Nahum prophesied specifically against the city of Nineveh, which was the capital of the Assyrian Empire. He warned of the coming destruction of the city and the downfall of the Assyrian empire as a whole, which would be brought about by the wrath of God. The book of Nahum portrays God as a just and righteous judge who will not tolerate the wickedness and cruelty of the Assyrians. It also provides a message of hope and comfort for the people of Judah, who were under threat from the Assyrian Empire at the time.

The historical context in which Nahum lived is important for understanding his message. The Assyrians were known for their brutality and cruelty, and their conquests had created a great deal of fear and instability in the region. Nahum's prophecy would have been seen as a message of hope for those who were suffering under Assyrian rule, and a warning to the Assyrians themselves that their actions would not go unpunished. It is a message that still resonates today, as people continue to grapple with issues of violence, oppression, and justice in our own time.

Importance

The book of Nahum is important in the Bible because it provides a prophetic message about the judgment of God against Nineveh, the capital city of Assyria. This message was significant for the people of Judah, who had suffered under the oppressive rule of Assyria for many years. Nahum's prophecy gave them hope that their enemy would be defeated and their suffering would come to an end.

Nahum's prophecy also highlights the sovereignty of God and His justice. It emphasizes that God is in control of all things, including the rise and fall of nations, and that He will not tolerate injustice and wickedness forever. This message is still relevant today as it reminds us of the importance of living justly and following God's commands.

Furthermore, the book of Nahum is significant because it provides a glimpse into the political and military landscape of the ancient Near East during the 7th century BC. It sheds light on the conflict between the powerful Assyrian Empire and the smaller kingdoms of Judah and Israel. It also highlights the brutality of war and the devastating effects it can have on both the conquerors and the conquered.

Structure and organization

The Book of Nahum is a short prophetic book in the Old Testament of the Bible, consisting of only three chapters.

The book is structured in two main parts: the first chapter describes God's anger towards Nineveh and its imminent destruction, and the second and third chapters describe the details of that destruction. The book begins with a vivid description of God's wrath and ends with a hymn of praise to God for his justice.

Despite its short length, the Book of Nahum is significant in its portrayal of

God's justice and power. It also serves as a warning to nations and individuals who may ignore God's warnings and commit acts of injustice and violence.

Major Themes

The book of Nahum contains a message of judgment against the city of Nineveh, the capital of the Assyrian Empire, for its cruelty and violence towards other nations, including Israel. The primary theme of the book is God's justice, as he executes judgment on those who have committed evil and oppressed his people. The book also speaks to God's faithfulness to his covenant and his willingness to defend his people against their enemies.

Another major theme in the book of Nahum is the sovereignty of God. Throughout the book, it is clear that God is in control of history and is working out his purposes through the nations. Despite the apparent power and strength of the Assyrians, Nahum affirms that God is ultimately in control and will bring about justice for his people.

The book of Nahum also contains messages of comfort and hope for God's people. Nahum assures the people of Judah that their enemies will be defeated and that God will restore their fortunes. This theme of restoration is particularly evident in the final chapter of the book, which speaks of the destruction of Nineveh and the freedom and security that God's people will experience as a result.

Overall, the book of Nahum serves as a reminder that God is just and sovereign, and that he will ultimately bring about justice and deliverance for his people.

Message of judgment

Here are some verses from the book of Nahum in the King James Version that convey the message of judgment:

1. "God is jealous, and the Lord revengeth; the Lord revengeth, and is furious; the Lord will take vengeance on his adversaries, and he reserveth

wrath for his enemies." - Nahum 1:2

2. "The Lord is slow to anger, and great in power, and will not at all acquit the wicked: the Lord hath his way in the whirlwind and in the storm, and the clouds are the dust of his feet." - Nahum 1:3
3. "Who can stand before his indignation? and who can abide in the fierceness of his anger? his fury is poured out like fire, and the rocks are thrown down by him." - Nahum 1:6
4. "Behold upon the mountains the feet of him that bringeth good tidings, that publisheth peace! O Judah, keep thy solemn feasts, perform thy vows: for the wicked shall no more pass through thee; he is utterly cut off." - Nahum 1:15
5. "For while they be folden together as thorns, and while they are drunken as drunkards, they shall be devoured as stubble fully dry." - Nahum 1:10
6. "All thy strong holds shall be like fig trees with the firstripe figs: if they be shaken, they shall even fall into the mouth of the eater." - Nahum 3:12

These verses portray a message of God's wrath and judgment against Nineveh and its people due to their wickedness and sins. The verses emphasize God's power, fury, and the inevitability of his judgment upon those who oppose him. The punishment that Nineveh will face is described as complete and total destruction, with the city's strongholds being destroyed like ripe figs falling into the mouth of the eater. However, the verses also provide hope for those who remain faithful to God, promising peace and protection for the people of Judah.

Sovereignty of God

Here are some verses from Nahum in the KJV that speak about the sovereignty of God:

1. "The LORD is slow to anger, and great in power, and will not at all acquit the wicked: the LORD hath his way in the whirlwind and in the storm,

and the clouds are the dust of his feet." - Nahum 1:3

2. "What do ye imagine against the LORD? he will make an utter end: affliction shall not rise up the second time." - Nahum 1:9
3. "The LORD hath given a commandment concerning thee, that no more of thy name be sown: out of the house of thy gods will I cut off the graven image and the molten image: I will make thy grave; for thou art vile." - Nahum 1:14
4. "Behold upon the mountains the feet of him that bringeth good tidings, that publisheth peace! O Judah, keep thy solemn feasts, perform thy vows: for the wicked shall no more pass through thee; he is utterly cut off." - Nahum 1:15

These verses show that God is in control of all things and has power over nature and the affairs of nations. They also emphasize God's justice and the fact that the wicked will be punished.

Messages of comfort and hope

The book of Nahum primarily focuses on the coming destruction of Nineveh, the capital city of the Assyrian Empire. However, it also includes messages of comfort and hope for Judah, who had suffered at the hands of the Assyrians. Here are some verses from Nahum that speak of this hope and comfort:

1. "The Lord is good, a stronghold in the day of trouble; and he knoweth them that trust in him" (Nahum 1:7).
2. "Behold upon the mountains the feet of him that bringeth good tidings, that publisheth peace! O Judah, keep thy solemn feasts, perform thy vows: for the wicked shall no more pass through thee; he is utterly cut off" (Nahum 1:15).
3. "And the Lord hath given a commandment concerning thee, that no more of thy name be sown: out of the house of thy gods will I cut off the graven image and the molten image: I will make thy grave; for thou art vile" (Nahum 1:14).

4. "For now will I break his yoke from off thee, and will burst thy bonds in sunder" (Nahum 1:13).
5. "The Lord will restore the splendor of Jacob like the splendor of Israel, though destroyers have laid them waste and have ruined their vines" (Nahum 2:2).
6. "The Lord will be awesome to them when he destroys all the gods of the earth. Distant nations will bow down to him, all of them in their own lands" (Nahum 1:6).

These verses remind the people of Judah that despite their current situation, God is still with them and will restore them. They also speak of the coming destruction of Nineveh, which would bring an end to the Assyrian oppression of Judah.

10

Zephaniah -Minor Prophet (640-609 BC)

The name "Zephaniah" means "Yahweh has hidden" or "Yahweh has treasured up" in Hebrew.

Zephaniah was a prophet in the southern kingdom of Judah who lived during the reign of King Josiah, around the 7th century BC. He was a contemporary of the prophets Jeremiah and Habakkuk. Zephaniah is believed to have been of royal lineage, possibly a descendant of King Hezekiah.

During Zephaniah's time, Judah was experiencing a period of moral and spiritual decline, marked by idolatry and social injustice. The nation was also under the threat of foreign invasion, with the Assyrian empire to the north and the rising Babylonian empire to the east.

Zephaniah's message focused on the themes of judgment and restoration. He warned of the impending judgment of God upon Judah and the surrounding nations, calling for repentance and a turning back to God. He also spoke of the hope of restoration and renewal for those who would turn to God and seek his ways. Overall, Zephaniah's message emphasized the sovereignty of God and the need for faithful obedience to his commands.

Historical and Cultural Context

Zephaniah was a prophet who lived in Judah during the reign of King Josiah in the late 7th century BC. At this time, Judah was experiencing a period of religious reform and revival under the leadership of King Josiah, who was seeking to rid the nation of idolatry and turn the people back to the worship of the one true God.

However, despite these efforts, the nation of Judah was still facing the threat of invasion and destruction from its neighboring nations, particularly the Assyrians and Babylonians. Zephaniah's prophecies reflect this context of political instability and the need for spiritual renewal.

Zephaniah's ministry likely took place during the latter part of Josiah's reign, around 640-609 BC. At this time, Judah was a small kingdom under the dominance of the powerful Assyrian empire. However, in the late 7th century BC, the Assyrian empire was beginning to decline, and new powers were rising in the region, including the Babylonians.

Zephaniah's prophecies warn of the impending judgment and destruction that would come upon Judah if the people did not turn back to God and repent of their sins. He also prophesied about the future restoration and renewal of the nation under the Messiah.

Importance

The book of Zephaniah is important in the Bible for its emphasis on the day of the Lord, a day of judgment and restoration, and its call to repentance and worship of the one true God. Zephaniah's message is particularly relevant to the people of Judah during his time, as they were guilty of idolatry and moral corruption, and facing the threat of invasion and destruction from foreign powers.

Zephaniah also emphasizes God's sovereignty and justice, and the importance of living in obedience and humility before Him. He prophesies about the judgment that will come upon the wicked and unrepentant, but also about the restoration and blessings that will come to the faithful and humble.

Overall, the book of Zephaniah is a reminder of the importance of repentance, faithfulness, and worship of the true God, and a warning of the consequences of disobedience and rebellion.

Structure and organization

The book of Zephaniah is organized into three chapters. The first chapter describes the coming judgment of the Lord upon Judah and Jerusalem for their sins of idolatry and social injustice. The second chapter speaks of the judgment upon the surrounding nations, particularly the neighboring city of Nineveh. The third chapter speaks of a future restoration and salvation of the remnant of Israel, with a call to rejoice and sing for joy.

Overall, the structure of the book is a call to repentance and a warning of judgment, followed by a promise of restoration and salvation for those who turn back to the Lord.

Major Themes

The major themes in the book of Zephaniah include:

1. The Day of the Lord: Zephaniah speaks of a coming day of judgment when God will punish the wicked and purify His people. This theme emphasizes the sovereignty of God and the need for people to turn from their sins.
2. Repentance and Judgment: The prophet calls for repentance from sin and disobedience, warning of the judgment that is to come. He urges the people to seek righteousness and humility before God.
3. Restoration and Salvation: Amid the warnings of judgment, Zephaniah offers hope for restoration and salvation. He speaks of a remnant of faithful people who will be saved, and the eventual restoration of God's people to their land.
4. The Character of God: Zephaniah emphasizes the character of God as holy, just, and merciful. He portrays God as a warrior who will fight for

His people and a shepherd who will gather and protect His flock.

5. Judgment against Nations: Zephaniah prophesies against other nations, including Assyria and Ethiopia, for their arrogance and mistreatment of God's people. This theme emphasizes the universal scope of God's plan and the need for all nations to repent and turn to Him.

The Day of the Lord

Zephaniah speaks about the "Day of the Lord," a term used to describe a time of divine judgment and reckoning. Here are some verses from Zephaniah on this theme in the King James Version (KJV):

1. "The great day of the Lord is near, it is near, and hasteth greatly, even the voice of the day of the Lord: the mighty man shall cry there bitterly." (Zephaniah 1:14)
2. "That day is a day of wrath, a day of trouble and distress, a day of wasteness and desolation, a day of darkness and gloominess, a day of clouds and thick darkness." (Zephaniah 1:15)
3. "And I will bring distress upon men, that they shall walk like blind men, because they have sinned against the Lord: and their blood shall be poured out as dust, and their flesh as the dung." (Zephaniah 1:17)
4. "The great day of the Lord is near, it is near, and hasteth greatly, even the voice of the day of the Lord: the mighty man shall cry there out bitterly." (Zephaniah 1:18)
5. "Therefore wait ye upon me, saith the Lord, until the day that I rise up to the prey: for my determination is to gather the nations, that I may assemble the kingdoms, to pour upon them mine indignation, even all my fierce anger: for all the earth shall be devoured with the fire of my jealousy." (Zephaniah 3:8)

In these verses, Zephaniah warns of a day of judgment that is coming, where God will bring wrath and punishment upon those who have sinned against Him. The language is vivid and apocalyptic, describing darkness, distress, and the pouring out of blood. However, there is also a call to wait upon the Lord and trust in His judgment, for He will gather the nations and assemble the kingdoms to pour out His indignation upon them. Ultimately, this day of the Lord will be a time of reckoning and purification for the earth.

Repentance and Judgment

Here are some verses from Zephaniah in the KJV that speak about repentance and judgment:

1. "Gather yourselves together, yea, gather together, O nation not desired; Before the decree bring forth, before the day pass as the chaff, before the fierce anger of the LORD come upon you, before the day of the LORD'S anger come upon you. Seek ye the LORD, all ye meek of the earth, which have wrought his judgment; seek righteousness, seek meekness: it may be ye shall be hid in the day of the LORD'S anger." (Zephaniah 2:1-3)
2. "I will also leave in the midst of thee an afflicted and poor people, and they shall trust in the name of the LORD. The remnant of Israel shall not do iniquity, nor speak lies; neither shall a deceitful tongue be found in their mouth: for they shall feed and lie down, and none shall make them afraid." (Zephaniah 3:12-13)
3. "Therefore wait ye upon me, saith the LORD, until the day that I rise up to the prey: for my determination is to gather the nations, that I may assemble the kingdoms, to pour upon them mine indignation, even all my fierce anger: for all the earth shall be devoured with the fire of my jealousy. For then will I turn to the people a pure language, that they may all call upon the name of the LORD, to serve him with one consent." (Zephaniah 3:8-9)

In these verses, Zephaniah urges his audience to seek the Lord, to trust in His name, and to repent of their sins. He also warns of the coming judgment of the Lord upon the nations and the earth, but promises that those who trust in the Lord and seek righteousness will be saved.

Restoration and Salvation

Here are some verses from the book of Zephaniah in the KJV that speak about restoration and salvation:

1. "The LORD thy God in the midst of thee is mighty; he will save, he will rejoice over thee with joy; he will rest in his love, he will joy over thee with singing." (Zephaniah 3:17)
2. "I will also leave in the midst of thee an afflicted and poor people, and they shall trust in the name of the LORD. The remnant of Israel shall not do iniquity, nor speak lies; neither shall a deceitful tongue be found in their mouth: for they shall feed and lie down, and none shall make them afraid." (Zephaniah 3:12-13)
3. "At that time will I bring you again, even in the time that I gather you: for I will make you a name and a praise among all people of the earth, when I turn back your captivity before your eyes, saith the LORD." (Zephaniah 3:20)

These verses speak about the salvation and restoration of God's people. Despite the judgment and punishment that they will face for their sins, God promises to save a remnant of faithful people and to restore them to their land. These verses also speak of the joy and singing that will accompany this restoration and salvation. Overall, the book of Zephaniah emphasizes the importance of turning back to God in repentance and faith, and the hope and assurance of salvation that can be found in Him.

The Character of God

Here are some verses in Zephaniah that speak of the character of God in the King James Version:

1. Zephaniah 3:5 - "The just Lord is in the midst thereof; he will not do iniquity: every morning doth he bring his judgment to light, he faileth

not; but the unjust knoweth no shame."

2. Zephaniah 3:17 - "The Lord thy God in the midst of thee is mighty; he will save, he will rejoice over thee with joy; he will rest in his love, he will joy over thee with singing."
3. Zephaniah 2:3 - "Seek ye the Lord, all ye meek of the earth, which have wrought his judgment; seek righteousness, seek meekness: it may be ye shall be hid in the day of the Lord's anger."
4. Zephaniah 3:9 - "For then will I turn to the people a pure language, that they may all call upon the name of the Lord, to serve him with one consent."
5. Zephaniah 3:14 - "Sing, O daughter of Zion; shout, O Israel; be glad and rejoice with all the heart, O daughter of Jerusalem."

These verses speak of God's justice, righteousness, love, and salvation. They also emphasize the importance of seeking and serving the Lord, and the joy and gladness that comes from being in relationship with Him.

Judgment against Nations

Here are some verses in Zephaniah that speak about God's judgment against nations:

1. "I will utterly consume all things from off the land, saith the Lord. I will consume man and beast; I will consume the fowls of the heaven, and the fishes of the sea, and the stumbling blocks with the wicked; and I will cut off man from off the land, saith the Lord." (Zephaniah 1:2–3)
2. "Therefore wait ye upon me, saith the Lord, until the day that I rise up to the prey: for my determination is to gather the nations, that I may assemble the kingdoms, to pour upon them mine indignation, even all my fierce anger: for all the earth shall be devoured with the fire of my jealousy." (Zephaniah 3:8)
3. "I have cut off the nations: their towers are desolate; I made their streets waste, that none passeth by: their cities are destroyed, so that there is

no man, that there is none inhabitant." (Zephaniah 3:6)

4. "For Gaza shall be forsaken, and Ashkelon a desolation: they shall drive out Ashdod at the noon day, and Ekron shall be rooted up. Woe unto the inhabitants of the sea coast, the nation of the Cherethites! the word of the Lord is against you; O Canaan, the land of the Philistines, I will even destroy thee, that there shall be no inhabitant." (Zephaniah 2:4-5)
5. "And I will bring distress upon men, that they shall walk like blind men, because they have sinned against the Lord: and their blood shall be poured out as dust, and their flesh as the dung. Neither their silver nor their gold shall be able to deliver them in the day of the Lord's wrath; but the whole land shall be devoured by the fire of his jealousy: for he shall make even a speedy riddance of all them that dwell in the land." (Zephaniah 1:17-18)

These verses speak of God's judgment against nations that have sinned against Him. The prophet warns of the coming day of the Lord when God will pour out His wrath on the wicked and destroy the nations that have rebelled against Him. The judgment will be so severe that even their wealth will not be able to save them. However, there is hope for those who turn to the Lord in repentance, as He promises restoration and salvation for those who seek Him.

11

Jeremiah - Major Prophet (627-586 BC)

The name "Jeremiah" means "Yahweh will exalt" or "Yahweh will uplift."

Jeremiah was a prophet in ancient Israel who lived during the late 7th and early 6th centuries BCE. He was born into a priestly family in the town of Anathoth, near Jerusalem. According to the Bible, Jeremiah began his prophetic ministry in the 13th year of King Josiah of Judah, around 627 BCE, and continued to prophesy until the fall of Jerusalem in 586 BCE and beyond.

Jeremiah lived in a time of great political upheaval and religious corruption. He witnessed the rise and fall of several kings of Judah, including Josiah, Jehoiakim, and Zedekiah, as well as the Babylonian conquest of Jerusalem and the subsequent exile of the Jewish people. Jeremiah's prophetic message focused on the need for repentance and faithfulness to God, as well as the consequences of disobedience and the hope of restoration.

Jeremiah's life and message were met with much opposition and persecution, as he often spoke out against the religious and political leaders of his day. He was imprisoned, beaten, and threatened with death, but he remained faithful to his calling and continued to proclaim the word of God until the end of his life. His prophecies and writings have had a profound influence on the Jewish and Christian faiths, and he is considered one of the major prophets of the Hebrew Bible.

Historical and Cultural Context

Jeremiah lived during a tumultuous time in ancient Israel's history. He was born around 650 BCE in Anathoth, a small village near Jerusalem, and began his ministry as a prophet during the reign of King Josiah. Josiah was a reformer who sought to rid the nation of idolatry and return it to a pure form of worship, but after his death, the kingdom was quickly thrown into turmoil.

Jeremiah witnessed the rise and fall of several kings of Judah, including Jehoahaz, Jehoiakim, and Zedekiah. He saw the nation come under the control of Babylon and was a firsthand witness to the destruction of Jerusalem and the temple in 586 BCE. During his ministry, Jeremiah prophesied that the nation would be punished for its sins, warned of the coming invasion by Babylon, and called for repentance and faithfulness to God.

Jeremiah's message was not well received by the people of Judah, who rejected him as a prophet and often persecuted him. Despite this, he continued to faithfully proclaim God's word and provide guidance and hope for the faithful remnant who listened to his message. His prophecies were recorded in the book of Jeremiah, which is one of the longest books in the Old Testament.

Importance

The book of Jeremiah is considered important in the Bible because it is one of the longest prophetic books, containing a detailed account of Jeremiah's ministry and the events that occurred during his time. The book presents a powerful message about the nature of God, the consequences of disobedience, and the hope of redemption and restoration.

Jeremiah's message of judgment and the impending destruction of Jerusalem and the Temple was fulfilled in 586 BC when the Babylonians conquered Judah and destroyed the city and the Temple. His message of hope and restoration, however, was also fulfilled when the exiles returned to Jerusalem and rebuilt the Temple.

The book of Jeremiah is also significant because it provides insights into the life and character of the prophet Jeremiah, who is often regarded as one of the most important figures in Jewish history. His prophetic call, his struggles with his own faith and doubts, and his unwavering commitment to the message he was called to deliver make him an inspiring and relatable figure for many readers.

Structure and organization

The book of Jeremiah is organized into 52 chapters and can be divided into three main sections:

1. The Call and Early Prophecies of Jeremiah (Chapters 1-25): This section includes the account of Jeremiah's call to prophesy, his early messages to the people of Judah, and his warnings of impending judgment if they did not repent.
2. The Prophecies Against the Nations (Chapters 26-45): This section contains prophecies against various nations, including Judah, as well as the account of Jeremiah's persecution and imprisonment.
3. The Historical Appendix (Chapters 46-52): This section includes prophecies against Egypt, Babylon, and other nations, as well as the account of the fall of Jerusalem to the Babylonians and the exile of the Jews to Babylon.

Major Themes

Some of the major themes in the book of Jeremiah include:

1. The impending judgment of God: Jeremiah prophesies the coming judgment of God upon Judah and its neighboring nations for their sins and disobedience.
2. The call to repentance: Despite the impending judgment, Jeremiah calls on the people to repent and turn back to God.
3. The sovereignty and faithfulness of God: Jeremiah emphasizes that God is in control of all things and that His promises will be fulfilled.

4. The role of the prophet: Jeremiah presents himself as a faithful prophet of God, called to speak truth to power and warn the people of God's judgment.
5. The importance of obedience: Throughout the book, Jeremiah emphasizes the importance of obeying God and following His commands.
6. The promise of restoration: In addition to the judgment, Jeremiah also prophesies a time of restoration and renewal for the people of God.
7. The Messiah and the new covenant: Jeremiah prophesies the coming of a Messiah and a new covenant between God and His people, which will bring about ultimate salvation and restoration.

The impending judgment of God

The call to repentance

Here are some verses in Jeremiah that discuss the call to repentance:

1. "Return, thou backsliding Israel, saith the Lord; and I will not cause mine anger to fall upon you: for I am merciful, saith the Lord, and I will not keep anger for ever." (Jeremiah 3:12)
2. "Thus saith the Lord of hosts, the God of Israel; Amend your ways and your doings, and I will cause you to dwell in this place." (Jeremiah 7:3)
3. "Therefore now amend your ways and your doings, and obey the voice of the Lord your God; and the Lord will repent him of the evil that he hath pronounced against you." (Jeremiah 26:13)
4. "O Jerusalem, wash thine heart from wickedness, that thou mayest be saved. How long shall thy vain thoughts lodge within thee?" (Jeremiah 4:14)
5. "Break up your fallow ground, and sow not among thorns. Circumcise yourselves to the Lord, and take away the foreskins of your heart, ye men of Judah and inhabitants of Jerusalem: lest my fury come forth like fire, and burn that none can quench it, because of the evil of your doings." (Jeremiah 4:3-4)

These verses emphasize the importance of repentance and turning away from sin, with the promise of God's mercy and forgiveness for those who do so.

The sovereignty and faithfulness of God

Here are some verses of The sovereignty and faithfulness of God in Jeremiah (KJV):

1. "Ah Lord God! behold, thou hast made the heaven and the earth by thy great power and stretched out arm, and there is nothing too hard for thee:" (Jeremiah 32:17)
2. "Thus saith the Lord, which giveth the sun for a light by day, and the ordinances of the moon and of the stars for a light by night, which divideth the sea when the waves thereof roar; The Lord of hosts is his name:" (Jeremiah 31:35)
3. "For I know the thoughts that I think toward you, saith the Lord, thoughts of peace, and not of evil, to give you an expected end." (Jeremiah 29:11)
4. "The Lord hath appeared of old unto me, saying, Yea, I have loved thee with an everlasting love: therefore with lovingkindness have I drawn thee." (Jeremiah 31:3)
5. "But the Lord is the true God, he is the living God, and an everlasting king: at his wrath the earth shall tremble, and the nations shall not be able to abide his indignation." (Jeremiah 10:10)

These verses demonstrate the sovereignty and faithfulness of God as the creator of the heavens and the earth, the one who controls the movements of the sun, moon, and stars, and the one who knows the plans he has for his people. They also show God's everlasting love and his power to bring judgment upon those who disobey him.

The role of the prophet

Here are some verses from Jeremiah that highlight the role of the prophet:

1. "Then the Lord put forth His hand and touched my mouth, and the Lord said to me: 'Behold, I have put My words in your mouth. See, I have this day set you over the nations and over the kingdoms, to root out and to pull down, to destroy and to throw down, to build and to plant.'" (Jeremiah 1:9-10)
2. "Thus says the Lord of hosts: 'Do not listen to the words of the prophets who prophesy to you. They make you worthless; they speak a vision of their own heart, not from the mouth of the Lord.'" (Jeremiah 23:16)
3. "For both prophet and priest are profane; yes, in My house I have found their wickedness," says the Lord. (Jeremiah 23:11)
4. "The prophet who has a dream, let him tell a dream; and he who has My word, let him speak My word faithfully. What is the chaff to the wheat?" says the Lord." (Jeremiah 23:28)
5. "Therefore thus says the Lord God of hosts: 'Because you speak this word, behold, I will make My words in your mouth fire, and this people wood, and it shall devour them.'" (Jeremiah 5:14)

These verses emphasize the important role of the prophet in conveying God's message to the people. The prophet is called by God to speak on His behalf, and their words are to be faithful and true. However, Jeremiah also acknowledges that there were false prophets who spoke visions of their own heart rather than from God, leading people astray. Ultimately, the prophet's role is to root out wickedness and call people to repentance, even if it means delivering a difficult message.

The importance of obedience

Here are some more verses on the importance of obedience in Jeremiah:

1. "But this thing commanded I them, saying, Obey my voice, and I will be your God, and ye shall be my people: and walk ye in all the ways that I have commanded you, that it may be well unto you." - Jeremiah 7:23
2. "Thus saith the Lord of hosts, the God of Israel; Amend your ways and your doings, and I will cause you to dwell in this place." - Jeremiah 7:3
3. "And it shall come to pass, if ye diligently hearken unto me, saith the Lord, to bring in no burden through the gates of this city on the sabbath day, but hallow the sabbath day, to do no work therein; Then shall there enter into the gates of this city kings and princes sitting upon the throne of David, riding in chariots and on horses, they, and their princes, the men of Judah, and the inhabitants of Jerusalem: and this city shall remain for ever." - Jeremiah 17:24-25
4. "And now therefore thus saith the Lord of hosts, the God of Israel; Wherefore commit ye this great evil against your souls, to cut off from you man and woman, child and suckling, out of Judah, to leave you none to remain;" - Jeremiah 44:7
5. "And it shall come to pass, when ye shall say, Wherefore doeth the Lord our God all these things unto us? then shalt thou answer them, Like as ye have forsaken me, and served strange gods in your land, so shall ye serve strangers in a land that is not yours." - Jeremiah 5:19
6. "Thus saith the Lord, Stand ye in the ways, and see, and ask for the old paths, where is the good way, and walk therein, and ye shall find rest for your souls. But they said, We will not walk therein." - Jeremiah 6:16
7. "But if ye will not hear it, my soul shall weep in secret places for your pride; and mine eye shall weep sore, and run down with tears, because the Lord's flock is carried away captive." - Jeremiah 13:17

The promise of restoration

Throughout the book of Jeremiah, there are numerous prophecies of judgment and condemnation against Judah for their disobedience and idolatry. However, even in the midst of these warnings, God promises a future restoration and redemption for His people.

- "For I know the thoughts that I think toward you, saith the Lord, thoughts of peace, and not of evil, to give you an expected end." (Jeremiah 29:11)
- "Therefore fear thou not, O my servant Jacob, saith the Lord; neither be dismayed, O Israel: for, lo, I will save thee from afar, and thy seed from the land of their captivity; and Jacob shall return, and shall be in rest, and be quiet, and none shall make him afraid." (Jeremiah 30:10)
- "Behold, I will bring it health and cure, and I will cure them, and will reveal unto them the abundance of peace and truth." (Jeremiah 33:6)

These promises of restoration and renewal in the book of Jeremiah point to the faithfulness and mercy of God, who desires to bring His people back to Himself despite their failures and disobedience. They offer hope and assurance to the faithful remnant of Israel, and serve as a reminder to us today of God's enduring love and steadfastness towards His people.

The Messiah and the new covenant

Some verses in Jeremiah that speak of the Messiah and the new covenant are:

- "Behold, the days are coming, declares the Lord, when I will raise up for David a righteous Branch, and he shall reign as king and deal wisely, and shall execute justice and righteousness in the land. In his days Judah will be saved, and Israel will dwell securely. And this is the name by which he will be called: 'The Lord is our righteousness'" (Jeremiah 23:5-6).
- "Behold, the days are coming, declares the Lord, when I will make a new covenant with the house of Israel and the house of Judah, not like the

covenant that I made with their fathers on the day when I took them by the hand to bring them out of the land of Egypt, my covenant that they broke, though I was their husband, declares the Lord. For this is the covenant that I will make with the house of Israel after those days, declares the Lord: I will put my law within them, and I will write it on their hearts. And I will be their God, and they shall be my people" (Jeremiah 31:31-33).

- "At that time, declares the Lord, I will be the God of all the clans of Israel, and they shall be my people. Thus says the Lord: 'The people who survived the sword found grace in the wilderness; when Israel sought for rest, the Lord appeared to him from far away. I have loved you with an everlasting love; therefore I have continued my faithfulness to you. Again I will build you, and you shall be built, O virgin Israel! Again you shall adorn yourself with tambourines and shall go forth in the dance of the merrymakers'" (Jeremiah 31:1-4).

12

Lamentations - Author Jeremiah (627-586 BC)

The word "Lamentations" means the passionate expression of grief or sorrow. It is derived from the Latin word "lamentationem," which means "wailing, weeping, or lamenting." In the context of the Bible, the Book of Lamentations is a collection of five poems that express profound grief and sorrow over the destruction of Jerusalem and the exile of the Israelites. The book is traditionally attributed to the prophet Jeremiah, who is believed to have written it in response to the Babylonian destruction of Jerusalem in 586 BCE.

Lamentations is a book of five poetic laments traditionally attributed to the prophet Jeremiah. The book mourns the destruction of Jerusalem and the Babylonian exile of the Jewish people. The author is unnamed, but the use of first-person throughout the book suggests that it may have been written by someone who personally witnessed the destruction. The most common understanding is that Jeremiah wrote Lamentations which is why Lamentations is counted as a Major Prophet.

The book is set in the aftermath of the Babylonian destruction of Jerusalem in 586 BCE. The city's walls were breached, the temple was destroyed, and many of the inhabitants were killed or taken into exile in Babylon. Lamentations mourns the loss of Jerusalem and the temple, and the exile of the Jewish people.

The book is traditionally read on the Jewish holiday of Tisha B'Av, which commemorates the destruction of both the first and second temples in Jerusalem. It is a powerful expression of grief and mourning, and it serves as a reminder of the consequences of turning away from God. Despite the book's somber tone, it also contains expressions of hope and a belief in God's mercy and compassion.

Historical and Cultural Context

The book of Lamentations is a poetic and emotional response to this catastrophic event, as it describes the devastation of the city, the suffering of the people, and the despair they felt. The author of the book speaks in the voice of the community, expressing their grief, anger, and hopelessness. The book also reflects the theological beliefs of the community, as they try to make sense of the disaster and understand their relationship with God.

The historical and cultural context of Lamentations is important because it provides a window into the experience of a community facing a profound crisis. The book offers insight into the emotional and spiritual responses of the people to this crisis, and into the theological ideas that sustained them in their suffering. Lamentations also highlights the importance of lament as a form of prayer and as a way of expressing faith in difficult times.

Importance

The book of Lamentations is important for several reasons. Firstly, it provides a vivid and emotionally powerful description of the destruction of Jerusalem by the Babylonians in 586 BC, and the resulting suffering and exile of the Jewish people. The book serves as a reminder of the consequences of disobedience to God and a call to repentance.

Secondly, the book of Lamentations is unique in its literary form. It is a collection of five poems, or laments, each consisting of 22 verses, with each verse beginning with a successive letter of the Hebrew alphabet. This structure gives the book a sense of order and unity, despite the chaotic subject matter.

Finally, the book of Lamentations has been traditionally associated with the prophet Jeremiah, who is believed to have written it. This association adds to the significance of the book, as Jeremiah is one of the most important prophets in the Old Testament, and his life and teachings are recorded in the book of Jeremiah.

Structure and Organization

The book of Lamentations consists of five chapters, each containing a poem or prayer of lament. The structure of the book can be divided into two parts:

1. Chapters 1-4 focus on the destruction of Jerusalem and the suffering of the people.
2. Chapter 5 is a prayer for restoration and mercy.

The poems are acrostics, meaning each verse or group of verses begins with a successive letter of the Hebrew alphabet. Chapters 1, 2, and 4 contain 22 verses each, corresponding to the 22 letters of the Hebrew alphabet. Chapter 3 has 66 verses, with three verses for each letter of the alphabet.

The book has a distinct structure that adds to its literary and emotional impact. It begins with a funeral dirge over the destruction of Jerusalem, progresses to a description of the horrific events, moves to a confession of sin, and ends with a prayer for deliverance and restoration.

Major Themes

The book of Lamentations is a collection of five poems that mourn the destruction of Jerusalem and the Babylonian exile of the people of Judah. Some of the major themes and messages of Lamentations include:

1. Mourning and grief: The book of Lamentations is a lament over the destruction of Jerusalem and the exile of the people of Judah. The poems express deep sadness, grief, and mourning over the loss of the city, the

Temple, and the people's way of life.

2. Confession of sin: The book of Lamentations also contains a confession of sin and guilt on behalf of the people of Judah. The poems acknowledge that the destruction of Jerusalem was a result of the people's disobedience and rebellion against God.
3. Hope in the midst of suffering: Despite the deep sadness and despair expressed in Lamentations, there are also moments of hope and faith. The poems express confidence in God's mercy and faithfulness, even in the midst of suffering and exile.
4. The justice of God: The book of Lamentations also acknowledges God's justice and the consequences of sin. The poems recognize that the destruction of Jerusalem was a result of God's judgment against the people's disobedience and rebellion.
5. The importance of repentance: Lamentations emphasizes the importance of repentance and turning back to God. The poems encourage the people to acknowledge their sin and to seek God's forgiveness and restoration.

Overall, Lamentations serves as a reminder of the consequences of sin and disobedience, but also as a testimony to the enduring faithfulness of God even in the midst of suffering and sorrow.

Mourning and grief

Here are some verses from the book of Lamentations that speak about mourning and grief in the King James Version:

1. "How doth the city sit solitary, that was full of people! how is she become as a widow! she that was great among the nations, and princess among the provinces, how is she become tributary!" - Lamentations 1:1
2. "Judah is gone into captivity because of affliction, and because of great servitude: she dwelleth among the heathen, she findeth no rest: all her persecutors overtook her between the straits." - Lamentations 1:3

3. "The ways of Zion do mourn, because none come to the solemn feasts: all her gates are desolate: her priests sigh, her virgins are afflicted, and she is in bitterness." - Lamentations 1:4
4. "For these things I weep; mine eye, mine eye runneth down with water, because the comforter that should relieve my soul is far from me: my children are desolate, because the enemy prevailed." - Lamentations 1:16
5. "Mine eye trickleth down, and ceaseth not, without any intermission, Till the Lord look down, and behold from heaven." - Lamentations 3:49-50

These verses describe the grief and mourning of the author, who is believed to be the prophet Jeremiah, over the destruction of Jerusalem and the captivity of the Israelites. The book is written as a series of poetic laments, expressing deep sadness and sorrow over the devastation that has befallen the people. The verses speak to the emotional and spiritual pain experienced by the Israelites during this time, as they mourned the loss of their city, their temple, and their way of life.

Confession of sin

Here are some verses in the book of Lamentations that discuss the confession of sin:

1. Lamentations 1:18 - "The Lord is righteous, for I have rebelled against his commandment; hear, all you peoples, and behold my sorrow; my virgins and my young men have gone into captivity."
2. Lamentations 3:39 - "Why should a living man complain, a man, about the punishment of his sins?"
3. Lamentations 3:40-42 - "Let us test and examine our ways, and return to the Lord! Let us lift up our hearts and hands to God in heaven: 'We have transgressed and rebelled, and you have not forgiven.'"
4. Lamentations 5:7 - "Our fathers sinned, and are no more; and we bear their iniquities."

These verses reflect a deep sense of remorse and repentance for the sins that led to the destruction of Jerusalem. The speaker acknowledges their own rebellion against God and confesses the sins of their fathers. The book of Lamentations serves as a powerful reminder of the consequences of disobedience to God and the importance of confessing and turning away from sin.

Hope in the midst of suffering

Here are some verses from Lamentations that speak of hope in the midst of suffering in the King James Version (KJV):

1. "It is of the Lord's mercies that we are not consumed, because his compassions fail not. They are new every morning: great is thy faithfulness." (Lamentations 3:22-23)
2. "The Lord is good unto them that wait for him, to the soul that seeketh him. It is good that a man should both hope and quietly wait for the salvation of the Lord." (Lamentations 3:25-26)
3. "Thou hast heard my voice: hide not thine ear at my breathing, at my cry. Thou drewest near in the day that I called upon thee: thou saidst, Fear not." (Lamentations 3:56-57)
4. "The Lord will not cast off for ever: But though he cause grief, yet will he have compassion according to the multitude of his mercies." (Lamentations 3:31-32)
5. "Thou, O Lord, remainest for ever; thy throne from generation to generation. Wherefore dost thou forget us for ever, and forsake us so long time?" (Lamentations 5:19-20)

These verses speak of the unchanging nature of God and his mercy, even in times of suffering and despair. They encourage the reader to have faith in God's goodness and to trust in his salvation, even when it seems far away.

The justice of God

Here are some verses in Lamentations that speak about the justice of God, using the King James Version:

1. "The Lord is righteous; for I have rebelled against his commandment: hear, I pray you, all people, and behold my sorrow: my virgins and my young men are gone into captivity." (Lamentations 1:18)
2. "Thou, O Lord, remainest for ever; thy throne from generation to generation. Wherefore dost thou forget us for ever, and forsake us so long time? Turn thou us unto thee, O Lord, and we shall be turned; renew our days as of old." (Lamentations 5:19-21)
3. "The Lord hath done that which he had devised; he hath fulfilled his word that he had commanded in the days of old: he hath thrown down, and hath not pitied: and he hath caused thine enemy to rejoice over thee, he hath set up the horn of thine adversaries." (Lamentations 2:17)
4. "The Lord is good unto them that wait for him, to the soul that seeketh him. It is good that a man should both hope and quietly wait for the salvation of the Lord." (Lamentations 3:25-26)
5. "Thou hast called as in a solemn day my terrors round about, so that in the day of the Lord's anger none escaped nor remained: those that I have swaddled and brought up hath mine enemy consumed." (Lamentations 2:22)

These verses speak of God's righteousness, faithfulness, and justice in fulfilling his word and bringing judgment upon the people for their sins. Yet, they also offer hope for those who seek God and wait for his salvation.

The importance of repentance

There are several verses in Lamentations that emphasize the importance of repentance. Here are a few examples in the King James Version:

1. "Let us search and try our ways, and turn again to the Lord." (Lamentations 3:40)
2. "Thou, O Lord, remainest for ever; thy throne from generation to generation. Wherefore dost thou forget us for ever, and forsake us so long time? Turn thou us unto thee, O Lord, and we shall be turned; renew our days as of old." (Lamentations 5:19-21)
3. "Let us lift up our heart with our hands unto God in the heavens. We have transgressed and have rebelled: thou hast not pardoned." (Lamentations 3:41-42)

These verses emphasize the need for the people to examine their ways, confess their sins, and turn back to the Lord in repentance. The book of Lamentations serves as a reminder that sin has consequences, but that God is merciful and will forgive those who turn back to Him.

13

Habakkuk - Minor Prophet (612-589 BC)

The name "Habakkuk" means "embrace" or "to cling to," suggesting a close relationship between the prophet and God. It may also be related to the Akkadian word "habbaquq," which means "plowman" or "gardener."

The prophet Habakkuk was likely a contemporary of Jeremiah, and his ministry took place in Judah before the Babylonian exile. Not much is known about Habakkuk's personal background, but his name means "embrace" or "wrestle" in Hebrew, and his book reflects his deep wrestling with God over the problem of evil and the apparent injustice in the world.

Habakkuk's ministry took place during a time of political and spiritual turmoil in Judah, as the nation was threatened by the rising power of Babylon and many people had turned away from God. In the midst of this difficult context, Habakkuk cried out to God and questioned why He allowed evil to go unpunished and why He appeared to be silent in the face of Judah's unfaithfulness.

Despite his struggles, Habakkuk ultimately came to a place of trust and faith in God's sovereignty and justice, declaring that "the righteous shall live by his faith" (Habakkuk 2:4). His book serves as a powerful testimony to the importance of honest questioning and wrestling with God in times of confusion and hardship, as well as the ultimate faithfulness of God in the midst of suffering.

Historical and Cultural Context

Habakkuk is believed to have prophesied during the late seventh century BC, around the time of the Babylonian invasion of Judah. At this time, Judah was a vassal state under Assyrian rule, and the people of Judah were facing moral and spiritual decline. Habakkuk's prophecies addressed these issues and provided hope and encouragement to the people of Judah during this difficult time. The historical context also includes the rise of the Babylonian Empire and the eventual destruction of Jerusalem and the Temple in 586 BC.

Importance

The book of Habakkuk is important for several reasons. First, it provides a unique perspective on the problem of evil and suffering in the world, as Habakkuk questions why God allows the wicked to prosper and the righteous to suffer. Second, it emphasizes the importance of faith in God, even in the midst of difficult circumstances. Finally, it contains several significant prophecies, including the prophecy that "the earth will be filled with the knowledge of the glory of the Lord, as the waters cover the sea" (Habakkuk 2:14).

Overall, the book of Habakkuk offers a powerful message of hope and faith in the face of adversity, and it serves as a reminder of God's sovereignty and justice.

Structure and organization

The book of Habakkuk consists of three chapters. The first chapter is a dialogue between Habakkuk and God, where Habakkuk questions why God allows evil to exist in the world. The second chapter is a response from God, where He promises to judge the wicked and vindicate the righteous. The third chapter is a prayer of Habakkuk, expressing his trust in God's sovereignty and salvation.

The book is structured as a chiasm, where the first and third chapters reflect each other in theme and structure, with the second chapter at the center. The chiasm emphasizes the central message of the book, which is the assurance of God's justice and the call to trust in Him, even in the midst of difficult circumstances.

Major themes

The major themes of Habakkuk include:

1. The justice and sovereignty of God: Habakkuk questions why God allows evil and injustice to continue, and God responds by affirming His sovereignty and His plans for justice.
2. The problem of evil: Habakkuk struggles with the problem of evil, and asks God why He allows the wicked to prosper and the righteous to suffer.
3. Faith and trust in God: Habakkuk ultimately resolves to trust in God's character and promises, even when circumstances seem bleak.
4. Judgment and punishment: Habakkuk prophesies that God will judge and punish the wicked nations, including Judah.
5. The salvation of the righteous: Habakkuk affirms that God will save and deliver the righteous, despite the trials and tribulations they may face.

The justice and sovereignty of God

Here are some verses from the book of Habakkuk that speak about the justice and sovereignty of God, in the King James Version (KJV):

1. "O LORD, how long shall I cry, and thou wilt not hear! even cry out unto thee of violence, and thou wilt not save!" - Habakkuk 1:2
2. "The LORD is slow to anger, and great in power, and will not at all acquit the wicked: the LORD hath his way in the whirlwind and in the storm, and the clouds are the dust of his feet." - Habakkuk 1:3
3. "Thou art of purer eyes than to behold evil, and canst not look on iniquity: wherefore lookest thou upon them that deal treacherously, and holdest

thy tongue when the wicked devoureth the man that is more righteous than he?" - Habakkuk 1:13

4. "Behold, his soul which is lifted up is not upright in him: but the just shall live by his faith." - Habakkuk 2:4
5. "For the earth shall be filled with the knowledge of the glory of the LORD, as the waters cover the sea." - Habakkuk 2:14
6. "O LORD, I have heard thy speech, and was afraid: O LORD, revive thy work in the midst of the years, in the midst of the years make known; in wrath remember mercy." - Habakkuk 3:2
7. "Although the fig tree shall not blossom, neither shall fruit be in the vines; the labour of the olive shall fail, and the fields shall yield no meat; the flock shall be cut off from the fold, and there shall be no herd in the stalls: Yet I will rejoice in the LORD, I will joy in the God of my salvation." - Habakkuk 3:17-18

These verses speak to the justice and sovereignty of God in various ways, including His power over nature and the fate of the wicked, His purity and righteousness, and the importance of living by faith. They also express the prophet's awe and fear of God, as well as his trust in Him even in the midst of difficult circumstances.

The problem of evil

Habakkuk asks questions about the justice of God and why He allows wickedness to go unpunished. Some verses that touch on these themes are:

- Habakkuk 1:2-4: "How long, Lord, must I call for help, but you do not listen? Or cry out to you, 'Violence!' but you do not save? Why do you make me look at injustice? Why do you tolerate wrongdoing? Destruction and violence are before me; there is strife, and conflict abounds. Therefore the law is paralyzed, and justice never prevails. The wicked hem in the righteous, so that justice is perverted."
- Habakkuk 1:13: "Your eyes are too pure to look on evil; you cannot

tolerate wrongdoing. Why then do you tolerate the treacherous? Why are you silent while the wicked swallow up those more righteous than themselves?"

- Habakkuk 2:3: "For the revelation awaits an appointed time; it speaks of the end and will not prove false. Though it linger, wait for it; it will certainly come and will not delay."
- Habakkuk 2:12: "Woe to him who builds a city with bloodshed and establishes a town by injustice!"
- Habakkuk 3:17-18: "Though the fig tree does not bud and there are no grapes on the vines, though the olive crop fails and the fields produce no food, though there are no sheep in the pen and no cattle in the stalls, yet I will rejoice in the Lord, I will be joyful in God my Savior."

Faith and trust in God

Here are some verses in Habakkuk that speak about faith and trust in God:

1. "The just shall live by his faith." - Habakkuk 2:4 (KJV)
2. "Although the fig tree shall not blossom, neither shall fruit be in the vines; the labour of the olive shall fail, and the fields shall yield no meat; the flock shall be cut off from the fold, and there shall be no herd in the stalls: Yet I will rejoice in the Lord, I will joy in the God of my salvation." - Habakkuk 3:17-18 (KJV)
3. "The Lord God is my strength, and he will make my feet like hinds' feet, and he will make me to walk upon mine high places." - Habakkuk 3:19 (KJV)

Judgment and punishment

Here are some verses in Habakkuk that deal with judgment and punishment:

1. "Why dost thou shew me iniquity, and cause me to behold grievance? for spoiling and violence are before me: and there are that raise up strife

and contention." - Habakkuk 1:3 (KJV)

2. "Therefore the law is slacked, and judgment doth never go forth: for the wicked doth compass about the righteous; therefore wrong judgment proceedeth." - Habakkuk 1:4 (KJV)
3. "Behold ye among the heathen, and regard, and wonder marvelously: for I will work a work in your days which ye will not believe, though it be told you." - Habakkuk 1:5 (KJV)
4. "For, lo, I raise up the Chaldeans, that bitter and hasty nation, which shall march through the breadth of the land, to possess the dwellingplaces that are not theirs." - Habakkuk 1:6 (KJV)
5. "They are terrible and dreadful: their judgment and their dignity shall proceed of themselves." - Habakkuk 1:7 (KJV)
6. "Their horses also are swifter than the leopards, and are more fierce than the evening wolves: and their horsemen shall spread themselves, and their horsemen shall come from far; they shall fly as the eagle that hasteth to eat." - Habakkuk 1:8 (KJV)
7. "Then shall his mind change, and he shall pass over, and offend, imputing this his power unto his god." - Habakkuk 1:11 (KJV)
8. "Art thou not from everlasting, O Lord my God, mine Holy One? we shall not die. O Lord, thou hast ordained them for judgment; and, O mighty God, thou hast established them for correction." - Habakkuk 1:12 (KJV)
9. "Thou art of purer eyes than to behold evil, and canst not look on iniquity: wherefore lookest thou upon them that deal treacherously, and holdest thy tongue when the wicked devoureth the man that is more righteous than he?" - Habakkuk 1:13 (KJV)
10. "Therefore they sacrifice unto their net, and burn incense unto their drag; because by them their portion is fat, and their meat plenteous." - Habakkuk 1:16 (KJV)

The salvation of the righteous

Here are some verses from Habakkuk that speak about the salvation of the righteous in the KJV translation:

1. "Behold, his soul which is lifted up is not upright in him: but the just shall live by his faith." - Habakkuk 2:4
2. "O Lord, I have heard thy speech, and was afraid: O Lord, revive thy work in the midst of the years, in the midst of the years make known; in wrath remember mercy." - Habakkuk 3:2
3. "Although the fig tree shall not blossom, neither shall fruit be in the vines; the labour of the olive shall fail, and the fields shall yield no meat; the flock shall be cut off from the fold, and there shall be no herd in the stalls: Yet I will rejoice in the Lord, I will joy in the God of my salvation." - Habakkuk 3:17-18
4. "The Lord God is my strength, and he will make my feet like hinds' feet, and he will make me to walk upon mine high places. To the chief singer on my stringed instruments." - Habakkuk 3:19

14

Ezekiel - Major Prophet (593-571 BC)

The name Ezekiel means "God strengthens" or "strengthened by God". It is of Hebrew origin and is derived from the words "hezeq", meaning "to strengthen", and "el", meaning "God"

Ezekiel was a prophet in ancient Israel and is known for the book that bears his name in the Old Testament. He lived during a time of great upheaval in Jewish history, as the Babylonian Empire was in the process of conquering the Kingdom of Judah and exiling many of its people to Babylon. Ezekiel was himself among those exiles, and his prophetic ministry took place during his time in Babylon.

Ezekiel was likely born into a priestly family and was trained as a priest himself. He began his prophetic ministry at the age of 30, around the same time that he and many other Jewish leaders were taken into exile in Babylon. His ministry lasted for around 22 years, during which time he received many visions and messages from God.

Ezekiel's message was primarily one of warning and judgment, as he called on the people of Judah to repent of their sins and turn back to God. He also offered messages of hope and restoration, promising that God would one day restore his people to their land and bless them once again. The book of Ezekiel is a powerful and complex work, filled with symbolic visions and prophetic pronouncements, and it continues to be studied and interpreted by scholars and believers today.

Historical and cultural context

Ezekiel was a Jewish priest and prophet who lived during the Babylonian exile, which lasted from 587 to 539 BCE. He was among the Jewish people who were exiled to Babylon by King Nebuchadnezzar II after he destroyed the city of Jerusalem and the First Temple in 586 BCE. During the exile, the Jewish people struggled with the loss of their land, their religious institutions, and their identity as a people. In this context, Ezekiel was called by God to serve as a prophet to the Jewish exiles.

Ezekiel's prophetic ministry began around 593 BCE, when he was 30 years old. He lived among the exiles in the city of Tel Abib on the banks of the Chebar River in Babylon. His prophecies were directed to the Jewish people in exile, as well as to the nations surrounding them. Ezekiel's ministry continued throughout the exile and beyond, until around 570 BCE, when the exiles began to return to their homeland under the Persian king Cyrus the Great.

During Ezekiel's time, the Jewish people were in a state of spiritual and moral decline. They had turned away from God and had been unfaithful to the covenant that God had made with them. They had also been influenced by the polytheistic religions of the Babylonians and other nations. In this context, Ezekiel's prophetic message focused on the themes of sin, judgment, and the need for repentance and restoration. He also emphasized the sovereignty and holiness of God, and the promise of a new covenant that would be established with the people of Israel.

Importance

The book of Ezekiel is significant in the Bible for its detailed prophecies, apocalyptic visions, and messages of judgment and restoration. Ezekiel's ministry took place during the Babylonian exile, when the Jewish people were exiled from their land and their temple was destroyed. Through Ezekiel, God delivered messages of judgment to the exiled people for their idolatry and disobedience, but also promised a future restoration of Israel and a new temple.

The book of Ezekiel also contains detailed prophecies about the coming of the Messiah and the establishment of God's kingdom. These prophecies were fulfilled in the life, death, and resurrection of Jesus Christ. Additionally, Ezekiel's visionary descriptions of the new temple and the river of life in chapters 40-48 have been interpreted as symbolic of the coming of the new heaven and new earth described in Revelation 21-22.

Overall, the book of Ezekiel emphasizes the holiness of God, the seriousness of sin, and the need for repentance and obedience. It also provides hope for a future restoration and the fulfillment of God's promises.

Structure and Organization

The book of Ezekiel is divided into three main parts:

1. Chapters 1-24: Prophecies of Judgment Against Judah and Jerusalem
2. Chapters 25-32: Prophecies of Judgment Against the Nations
3. Chapters 33-48: Prophecies of Restoration and Renewal

Within each section, there are various visions, parables, and symbolic acts that Ezekiel uses to communicate his message. The book also includes a detailed description of a future temple and its worship, as well as an extended vision of the valley of dry bones, which symbolizes Israel's restoration. The book ends with a description of a new city and a new temple in Israel.

Overall, the book of Ezekiel presents a powerful message of God's sovereignty, justice, and mercy, as well as the importance of repentance, obedience, and true worship. It is a significant prophetic book that speaks to both the people of Israel and the nations of the world.

Major Themes

The book of Ezekiel contains several major themes, including:

1. The Glory of God: One of the primary themes of Ezekiel is the glory of

God. Ezekiel has several visions of God's glory, including the famous vision of the "wheel within a wheel" (Ezekiel 1:4-28) and the vision of the restored temple (Ezekiel 43:1-5).

2. Sin and Judgment: Ezekiel also emphasizes the sinfulness of the people of Israel and the judgment that God will bring upon them. The book includes several prophecies of destruction and exile, as well as warnings to turn away from sin and seek God's forgiveness.
3. Restoration and Hope: Despite the judgment that God will bring upon Israel, Ezekiel also provides a message of hope and restoration. The book includes prophecies of the restoration of the temple and the land of Israel, as well as a vision of the valley of dry bones, which symbolizes the restoration of the people of Israel (Ezekiel 37:1-14).
4. The Role of the Prophet: Ezekiel's own life and ministry also serve as a theme of the book. God calls Ezekiel to be a watchman for the people of Israel, warning them of the impending judgment and calling them to repentance. Ezekiel's experiences and visions also serve as a model for the role of the prophet in Israel.
5. The Sovereignty of God: Throughout the book of Ezekiel, God's sovereignty is emphasized. God is in control of all things, even the judgment that he brings upon his people. Ezekiel teaches that God's sovereignty is a source of comfort and hope, even in the midst of difficult circumstances.

The Glory of God

Ezekiel is full of verses that speak about the glory of God. Here are some examples in the KJV:

1. "And above the firmament that was over their heads was the likeness of a throne, as the appearance of a sapphire stone: and upon the likeness of the throne was the likeness as the appearance of a man above upon it. And I saw as the colour of amber, as the appearance of fire round about within it, from the appearance of his loins even upward, and from the

appearance of his loins even downward, I saw as it were the appearance of fire, and it had brightness round about." (Ezekiel 1:26-27)

2. "And the glory of the LORD came into the house by the way of the gate whose prospect is toward the east." (Ezekiel 43:4)
3. "And the spirit took me up, and brought me into the inner court; and, behold, the glory of the LORD filled the house." (Ezekiel 43:5)
4. "Then I fell upon my face, and cried with a loud voice, and said, Ah Lord GOD! wilt thou make a full end of the remnant of Israel?" (Ezekiel 11:13)
5. "And the glory of the LORD went up from the midst of the city, and stood upon the mountain which is on the east side of the city." (Ezekiel 11:23)

These verses depict the majesty and splendor of God and the awe and reverence that should be given to Him. They show that God's glory is not just a concept but a tangible reality that can be experienced and witnessed.

Sin and Judgment

Here are some verses in the book of Ezekiel about sin and judgment in the King James Version:

1. "The soul that sinneth, it shall die. The son shall not bear the iniquity of the father, neither shall the father bear the iniquity of the son: the righteousness of the righteous shall be upon him, and the wickedness of the wicked shall be upon him." - Ezekiel 18:20
2. "Therefore I will judge you, O house of Israel, every one according to his ways, saith the Lord God. Repent, and turn yourselves from all your transgressions; so iniquity shall not be your ruin." - Ezekiel 18:30
3. "Say unto them, As I live, saith the Lord God, I have no pleasure in the death of the wicked; but that the wicked turn from his way and live: turn ye, turn ye from your evil ways; for why will ye die, O house of Israel?" - Ezekiel 33:11
4. "The Lord is slow to anger, and great in power, and will not at all acquit the wicked: the Lord hath his way in the whirlwind and in the storm, and

the clouds are the dust of his feet." - Ezekiel 32:30

5. "For thus saith the Lord God; How much more when I send my four sore judgments upon Jerusalem, the sword, and the famine, and the noisome beast, and the pestilence, to cut off from it man and beast?" - Ezekiel 14:21

These verses show that God is just and will judge sin, but He also desires for people to turn from their wicked ways and live. He takes no pleasure in the death of the wicked and warns them of the consequences of their actions. The book of Ezekiel emphasizes the importance of repentance and turning away from sin to avoid God's judgment.

Restoration and Hope

1. "Therefore say, Thus saith the Lord God; I will even gather you from the people, and assemble you out of the countries where ye have been scattered, and I will give you the land of Israel." (Ezekiel 11:17)
2. "For thus saith the Lord God; Behold, I, even I, will both search my sheep, and seek them out. As a shepherd seeketh out his flock in the day that he is among his sheep that are scattered; so will I seek out my sheep, and will deliver them out of all places where they have been scattered in the cloudy and dark day." (Ezekiel 34:11-12)
3. "Then will I sprinkle clean water upon you, and ye shall be clean: from all your filthiness, and from all your idols, will I cleanse you. A new heart also will I give you, and a new spirit will I put within you: and I will take away the stony heart out of your flesh, and I will give you an heart of flesh. And I will put my spirit within you, and cause you to walk in my statutes, and ye shall keep my judgments, and do them." (Ezekiel 36:25-27)
4. "And David my servant shall be king over them; and they all shall have one shepherd: they shall also walk in my judgments, and observe my statutes, and do them." (Ezekiel 37:24)
5. "And I will make them one nation in the land upon the mountains of Israel; and one king shall be king to them all: and they shall be no more

two nations, neither shall they be divided into two kingdoms any more at all." (Ezekiel 37:22)

These verses speak of God's promise to restore and renew His people, gathering them from exile and giving them a new heart and spirit, and unifying them under one king and one nation. They provide hope and encouragement to the Israelites during a time of great distress and uncertainty, assuring them of God's faithfulness and love.

The Role of the Prophet

Here are some verses in the book of Ezekiel that discuss the role of the prophet:

1. "Son of man, I have made thee a watchman unto the house of Israel: therefore hear the word at my mouth, and give them warning from me." (Ezekiel 3:17)
2. "So thou, O son of man, I have set thee a watchman unto the house of Israel; therefore thou shalt hear the word at my mouth, and warn them from me." (Ezekiel 33:7)
3. "Moreover he said unto me, Son of man, all my words that I shall speak unto thee receive in thine heart, and hear with thine ears. And go, get thee to them of the captivity, unto the children of thy people, and speak unto them, and tell them, Thus saith the Lord God; whether they will hear, or whether they will forbear." (Ezekiel 3:10–11)
4. "And they shall know that a prophet hath been among them." (Ezekiel 2:5)

These verses emphasize the role of the prophet as a messenger of God, responsible for warning and instructing the people according to the word of God. The prophet is called to receive God's word and to share it with the people, whether or not they choose to listen. The prophet is also a sign to the people, a symbol of God's presence and his desire to communicate with them.

The Sovereignty of God

Here are some verses from the book of Ezekiel that speak about the sovereignty of God, in the King James Version:

1. "Then I looked, and behold, a whirlwind was coming out of the north, a great cloud with raging fire engulfing itself; and brightness was all around it and radiating out of its midst like the color of amber, out of the midst of the fire. Also from within it came the likeness of four living creatures. And this was their appearance: they had the likeness of a man" (Ezekiel 1:4-5).
2. "And the hand of the LORD was upon me there. And He said to me, 'Arise, go out into the plain, and there I shall talk with you.' So I arose and went out into the plain, and behold, the glory of the LORD stood there, like the glory which I saw by the River Chebar; and I fell on my face" (Ezekiel 3:22-23).
3. "For thus says the Lord GOD: 'Indeed I Myself will search for My sheep and seek them out. As a shepherd seeks out his flock on the day he is among his scattered sheep, so will I seek out My sheep and deliver them from all the places where they were scattered on a cloudy and dark day'" (Ezekiel 34:11-12).
4. "Thus says the Lord GOD: 'When I have gathered the house of Israel from the peoples among whom they are scattered, and am hallowed in them in the sight of the Gentiles, then they will dwell in their own land which I gave to My servant Jacob. And they will dwell safely there, build houses, and plant vineyards; yes, they will dwell securely, when I execute judgments on all those around them who despise them. Then they shall know that I am the LORD their God'" (Ezekiel 28:25-26).
5. "Therefore thus says the Lord GOD: 'Behold, I lay in Zion a stone for a foundation, a tried stone, a precious cornerstone, a sure foundation; whoever believes will not act hastily'" (Ezekiel 28:16).

These verses and many others in the book of Ezekiel emphasize the sovereignty of God, his power and glory, his care for his people, and his plan for their restoration and salvation. Ezekiel also reveals God's justice and judgment, especially against those who have rebelled against him and oppressed his people. The role of the prophet in Ezekiel is to communicate God's messages to the people, to call them to repentance and faithfulness, and to assure them of God's promises of hope and restoration.

15

Daniel - Major Prophet (605-536 BC)

Daniel was a Jewish prophet who lived in Babylon during the 6th century BC. He was born in Jerusalem and was taken into captivity by King Nebuchadnezzar when he invaded Judah in 605 BC. As a young man, Daniel was selected along with other young Jewish men to be trained for service in the royal court of Babylon. Despite being in a foreign land, Daniel remained faithful to his God and was known for his wisdom, integrity, and spiritual discernment.

Daniel's prophetic ministry spanned several decades, during which he served in the courts of several Babylonian and Persian kings, including Nebuchadnezzar, Belshazzar, Darius, and Cyrus. He was known for his ability to interpret dreams and visions, and his prophecies foretold events that would take place long after his own lifetime, including the rise and fall of empires and the coming of the Messiah.

Daniel's story is recorded in the biblical book of Daniel, which contains a mix of narratives and apocalyptic visions. The book is divided into two parts: the first six chapters contain stories about Daniel's life and ministry in Babylon, while the remaining six chapters contain apocalyptic visions and prophecies about the future of Israel and the world. The book of Daniel is considered one of the major prophetic books in the Old Testament and is highly regarded for its literary and theological significance.

Historical and Cultural Context

Daniel lived during the time of the Babylonian Empire, which conquered the Kingdom of Judah in 586 BCE and took many of its people, including Daniel, into captivity. Daniel was a young Jewish noble who was chosen to serve in the court of King Nebuchadnezzar in Babylon. He remained in Babylon during the reigns of several kings, including Belshazzar, and eventually served as an adviser to Darius the Mede, who conquered Babylon in 539 BCE.

During this time, the Jews were a minority in a foreign land, and they faced many challenges to their faith and way of life. They were forbidden from practicing many of their religious customs and were often persecuted for their beliefs. Daniel and his companions faced many trials and temptations during their time in Babylon, but they remained faithful to God and were blessed by him.

Daniel also lived during a time of great political upheaval and conflict, as various empires vied for power and dominance in the ancient Near East. He witnessed the rise and fall of several empires, including the Babylonian, Persian, and Greek empires, and he prophesied about the coming of the Messiah and the end of the world. His prophecies continue to be studied and debated by scholars and theologians today.

Importance

The book of Daniel is significant in the Bible for several reasons. Firstly, it presents a unique blend of historical narrative, prophecy, and apocalyptic literature. Secondly, it provides a powerful example of faithfulness and devotion to God in the face of persecution and opposition. Thirdly, it contains some of the most detailed and specific prophecies in the entire Old Testament, including the coming of the Messiah and the end of the world. Finally, the book of Daniel has had a profound impact on both Jewish and Christian theology, influencing beliefs about eschatology, the resurrection of the dead, and the nature of God's kingdom.

Structure and Organization

The book of Daniel is divided into two parts: the first part (chapters 1-6) consists of stories and narratives, while the second part (chapters 7-12) contains apocalyptic visions and prophecies.

In the first part, we see Daniel and his three friends, Shadrach, Meshach, and Abednego, taken captive from Judah to Babylon by King Nebuchadnezzar. Daniel serves in the court of the king and interprets his dreams and visions, while his friends are thrown into a fiery furnace for refusing to worship an idol.

The second part of the book contains four visions that Daniel receives, all of which focus on the future and God's ultimate victory over evil. The final vision, in chapter 12, includes a description of the resurrection of the dead and the final judgment.

Overall, the book of Daniel emphasizes the sovereignty of God over all human kingdoms and powers and the ultimate triumph of God's kingdom over all earthly kingdoms. It also encourages faithfulness in the face of persecution and hope in the midst of difficult circumstances.

Major Themes

The book of Daniel covers a range of themes, including:

1. Faithfulness in Exile: The book of Daniel highlights the importance of remaining faithful to God even in the midst of difficult circumstances. Daniel and his friends are taken into captivity in Babylon, where they face numerous challenges to their faith, including pressure to conform to Babylonian culture and worship false gods.
2. God's Sovereignty: The book of Daniel emphasizes God's sovereignty over all human kingdoms and rulers. It shows how God is ultimately in control of human history and uses even pagan rulers to accomplish his purposes.
3. Prophecy and Apocalyptic Literature: The book of Daniel contains

numerous prophecies about the future, including the coming of the Messiah, the rise and fall of empires, and the end of the world. These prophecies are often presented in highly symbolic and apocalyptic language.

4. Divine Judgment: The book of Daniel also emphasizes the idea of divine judgment, both on individual sinners and on nations. It shows how God punishes those who rebel against him and how his judgment ultimately brings about justice and redemption.
5. Courage and Perseverance: The book of Daniel is also a story of courage and perseverance in the face of adversity. Daniel and his friends face numerous challenges to their faith and well-being, but they remain steadfast in their commitment to God and ultimately emerge as heroes and role models for future generations.

Faithfulness in Exile

Here are some verses from the book of Daniel that emphasize the theme of faithfulness in exile:

1. "But Daniel purposed in his heart that he would not defile himself with the portion of the king's meat, nor with the wine which he drank: therefore he requested of the prince of the eunuchs that he might not defile himself." (Daniel 1:8)
2. "Shadrach, Meshach, and Abednego, answered and said to the king, O Nebuchadnezzar, we are not careful to answer thee in this matter. If it be so, our God whom we serve is able to deliver us from the burning fiery furnace, and he will deliver us out of thine hand, O king. But if not, be it known unto thee, O king, that we will not serve thy gods, nor worship the golden image which thou hast set up." (Daniel 3:16-18)
3. "Then Daniel went to his house, and made the thing known to Hananiah, Mishael, and Azariah, his companions: That they would desire mercies of the God of heaven concerning this secret; that Daniel and his fellows should not perish with the rest of the wise men of Babylon." (Daniel

2:17–18)

4. "Then these men assembled unto the king, and said unto the king, Know, O king, that the law of the Medes and Persians is, That no decree nor statute which the king establisheth may be changed. Then the king commanded, and they brought Daniel, and cast him into the den of lions. Now the king spake and said unto Daniel, Thy God whom thou servest continually, he will deliver thee." (Daniel 6:15–16)

These verses illustrate the faithfulness of Daniel and his companions to their God even in the midst of a foreign land and hostile environment. They refused to compromise their beliefs and values, even when faced with persecution and death. Their unwavering faith and trust in God's sovereignty and power is a central theme throughout the book of Daniel.

God's Sovereignty

Here are some verses in the book of Daniel that speak of God's sovereignty, using the King James Version of the Bible:

1. "Blessed be the name of God for ever and ever: for wisdom and might are his: And he changeth the times and the seasons: he removeth kings, and setteth up kings: he giveth wisdom unto the wise, and knowledge to them that know understanding:" (Daniel 2:20–21)
2. "The king answered unto Daniel, and said, Of a truth it is, that your God is a God of gods, and a Lord of kings, and a revealer of secrets, seeing thou couldest reveal this secret." (Daniel 2:47)
3. "I saw in the night visions, and, behold, one like the Son of man came with the clouds of heaven, and came to the Ancient of days, and they brought him near before him. And there was given him dominion, and glory, and a kingdom, that all people, nations, and languages, should serve him: his dominion is an everlasting dominion, which shall not pass away, and his kingdom that which shall not be destroyed." (Daniel 7:13–14)

4. "He delivereth and rescueth, and he worketh signs and wonders in heaven and in earth, who hath delivered Daniel from the power of the lions." (Daniel 6:27)
5. "And at that time shall Michael stand up, the great prince which standeth for the children of thy people: and there shall be a time of trouble, such as never was since there was a nation even to that same time: and at that time thy people shall be delivered, every one that shall be found written in the book." (Daniel 12:1)

These verses demonstrate the theme of God's sovereignty in the book of Daniel, emphasizing His power and control over all things, including kings, nations, and even supernatural events. The book presents God as the ultimate authority and ruler of the universe, who has the power to protect His people and deliver them from danger. The themes of faithfulness and trust in God's sovereignty are also prominent throughout the book, as exemplified by Daniel and his companions who remained faithful to God in the face of persecution and adversity.

Prophecy and Apocalyptic Literature

Here are some verses from the book of Daniel that relate to prophecy and apocalyptic literature:

1. "Blessed be the name of God forever and ever, to whom belong wisdom and might." (Daniel 2:20, ESV)
2. "I saw in the night visions, and behold, with the clouds of heaven there came one like a son of man, and he came to the Ancient of Days and was presented before him. And to him was given dominion and glory and a kingdom, that all peoples, nations, and languages should serve him; his dominion is an everlasting dominion, which shall not pass away, and his kingdom one that shall not be destroyed." (Daniel 7:13-14, ESV)
3. "But the saints of the Most High shall receive the kingdom and possess the kingdom forever, forever and ever." (Daniel 7:18, ESV)

4. "At that time shall arise Michael, the great prince who has charge of your people. And there shall be a time of trouble, such as never has been since there was a nation till that time. But at that time your people shall be delivered, everyone whose name shall be found written in the book." (Daniel 12:1, ESV)
5. "And many of those who sleep in the dust of the earth shall awake, some to everlasting life, and some to shame and everlasting contempt. And those who are wise shall shine like the brightness of the sky above; and those who turn many to righteousness, like the stars forever and ever." (Daniel 12:2–3, ESV)

These verses demonstrate some of the prophetic and apocalyptic themes found in the book of Daniel, including the sovereignty of God, the coming of a messianic figure, the ultimate triumph of the saints, and the resurrection of the dead.

Divine Judgment

Here are some verses from the book of Daniel in the King James Version (KJV) that speak about divine judgment:

1. "As I looked, thrones were set in place, and the Ancient of Days took his seat. His clothing was as white as snow; the hair of his head was white like wool. His throne was flaming with fire, and its wheels were all ablaze." (Daniel 7:9)
2. "I watched as the beast was slain and its body destroyed and thrown into the blazing fire. (The other beasts had been stripped of their authority, but were allowed to live for a period of time.)" (Daniel 7:11–12)
3. "Then he said to me, "Do not be afraid, Daniel. Since the first day that you set your mind to gain understanding and to humble yourself before your God, your words were heard, and I have come in response to them." (Daniel 10:12)
4. "But the court will sit, and his power will be taken away and completely

destroyed forever." (Daniel 7:26)

5. "In my vision at night I looked, and there before me was one like a son of man, coming with the clouds of heaven. He approached the Ancient of Days and was led into his presence. He was given authority, glory and sovereign power; all nations and peoples of every language worshiped him. His dominion is an everlasting dominion that will not pass away, and his kingdom is one that will never be destroyed." (Daniel 7:13–14)

These verses speak of God's sovereignty and the judgment that comes with it. They show that God is the ultimate judge and that he will ultimately triumph over evil. The book of Daniel is full of prophetic visions and apocalyptic literature that reveal the future and God's plan for redemption and restoration.

Courage and Perseverance

Here are some verses on courage and perseverance from the book of Daniel in the King James Version:

1. "But Daniel purposed in his heart that he would not defile himself with the portion of the king's meat, nor with the wine which he drank: therefore he requested of the prince of the eunuchs that he might not defile himself." - Daniel 1:8
2. "Now when Daniel knew that the writing was signed, he went into his house; and his windows being open in his chamber toward Jerusalem, he kneeled upon his knees three times a day, and prayed, and gave thanks before his God, as he did aforetime." - Daniel 6:10
3. "And at that time shall Michael stand up, the great prince which standeth for the children of thy people: and there shall be a time of trouble, such as never was since there was a nation even to that same time: and at that time thy people shall be delivered, every one that shall be found written in the book." - Daniel 12:1
4. "But the people that do know their God shall be strong, and do exploits." - Daniel 11:32

5. "Many shall be purified, and made white, and tried; but the wicked shall do wickedly: and none of the wicked shall understand; but the wise shall understand." - Daniel 12:10

These verses encourage readers to remain faithful to God even in the face of adversity and persecution, and to trust in His power and sovereignty to deliver His people. The example of Daniel standing firm in his convictions, even when it meant going against the cultural norms of his time, inspires believers to have courage and integrity in the face of temptation. The prophecies of future trials and tribulations can also give hope and strength to those who trust in God's promises of deliverance and salvation.

16

Haggai - Minor Prophet (520 BC)

Haggai was one of the twelve minor prophets in the Old Testament of the Bible. He was a prophet in the early years of the Persian Empire and is believed to have been active from around 520-518 BCE. Haggai was a contemporary of the prophets Zechariah and Malachi, and he was a contemporary of the Jewish governor of Jerusalem, Zerubbabel, and the high priest Joshua.

Haggai lived during a time of great turmoil in Jewish history. The Jews had returned to Jerusalem after their exile in Babylon and were trying to rebuild their temple and their city. However, they faced opposition from their neighbors and lacked the resources and motivation to complete the work. Haggai's prophecies urged the people to complete the temple, and he encouraged them by promising that God would bless them if they did.

Haggai's message was an important one for the Jews of his time, as it helped them to refocus on their religious and cultural identity and to persevere in the face of adversity. His prophecies also had an enduring impact on later Jewish and Christian theology, as they helped to shape ideas about the nature of God and the importance of faith and obedience.

Historical and Cultural Context

The prophet Haggai lived during the time of the restoration of Jerusalem and the rebuilding of the temple after the Babylonian exile. In 586 BC, the Babylonians had destroyed the temple and taken many Jews into captivity. However, in 538 BC, King Cyrus of Persia issued a decree allowing the Jews to return to their homeland and rebuild the temple.

The Jews who returned to Jerusalem faced many challenges, including opposition from neighboring peoples, lack of resources, and apathy among the people. Haggai was one of the prophets sent by God to encourage the people to rebuild the temple and to remind them of God's faithfulness to his covenant with them.

Haggai's prophecies were given over a four-month period in 520 BC, and they were primarily focused on urging the people to complete the rebuilding of the temple. Haggai's message was not only one of encouragement but also of warning that the people's neglect of the temple was a reflection of their spiritual apathy and disobedience to God.

Importance

The book of Haggai is important because it encourages the Israelites to rebuild the temple, which had been destroyed during the Babylonian exile. The rebuilding of the temple was important for the Israelites because it was a symbol of their identity as God's people and their covenant relationship with Him. The book also emphasizes the need for the Israelites to prioritize God and His work, rather than focusing solely on their own needs and desires.

Additionally, the book of Haggai serves as a reminder of God's faithfulness and provision for His people, even in difficult and challenging circumstances. It also highlights the importance of obedience to God's commands and the blessings that come from following Him.

Overall, the book of Haggai provides important lessons and encouragement for believers today in their pursuit of God and His purposes.

Structure and organization

The book of Haggai consists of four chapters, with the following structure:

1. The first message and response (1:1-15)
2. The second message and response (2:1-9)
3. The third message and response (2:10-19)
4. The fourth message and response (2:20-23)

Each message consists of a message from God delivered by the prophet Haggai, followed by a response from the people. The book is organized in a way that emphasizes the importance of rebuilding the temple in Jerusalem, which had been destroyed by the Babylonians. The first message encourages the people to begin the work of rebuilding, while the second message reassures them of God's presence and promises to bless them. The third message reminds the people of the consequences of their disobedience in the past, and the fourth message prophesies about the future glory of the temple.

Major Themes

The major themes in the book of Haggai include:

1. The importance of rebuilding the temple: Haggai emphasizes the importance of rebuilding the temple in Jerusalem, which had been destroyed by the Babylonians. He urges the people to prioritize this task over their personal interests and encourages them with the promise of God's blessing if they obey.
2. The need for repentance: Haggai challenges the people to consider their ways and repent from their disobedience to God. He calls them to turn away from their selfishness and idolatry and to pursue righteousness and obedience to God.
3. The sovereignty and faithfulness of God: Haggai emphasizes God's sovereignty over all things and His faithfulness to His promises. He

reminds the people that God is in control of history and will keep His covenant promises to them.

4. The promise of future glory: Haggai encourages the people with the promise of future glory, both in terms of the rebuilding of the temple and the coming of the Messiah. He assures them that God will bless them and bring them peace, and that He will ultimately bring about the redemption of His people.
5. The role of the prophet: Haggai serves as a model of faithful prophetic ministry, calling the people to repentance and obedience to God's will. He demonstrates the importance of hearing and responding to the voice of God, and the power of prophetic words to bring about change in people's lives.

The importance of rebuilding the temple

"Hagai 1:2-9" in KJV says:

"Thus speaketh the Lord of hosts, saying, This people say, The time is not come, the time that the Lord's house should be built. Then came the word of the Lord by Haggai the prophet, saying, Is it time for you, O ye, to dwell in your ceiled houses, and this house lie waste? Now therefore thus saith the Lord of hosts; Consider your ways. Ye have sown much, and bring in little; ye eat, but ye have not enough; ye drink, but ye are not filled with drink; ye clothe you, but there is none warm; and he that earneth wages earneth wages to put it into a bag with holes. Thus saith the Lord of hosts; Consider your ways. Go up to the mountain, and bring wood, and build the house; and I will take pleasure in it, and I will be glorified, saith the Lord."

These verses emphasize the importance of rebuilding the temple which had been destroyed, and the message to the people to stop neglecting the rebuilding of the temple in favor of their own personal comforts. The prophet Haggai was sent by God to encourage the people to finish rebuilding the temple, which was an important symbol of God's presence among them. The people were reminded of their covenant with God and their responsibility to keep His commandments, including the rebuilding of the temple. Through this message, God promised to bless them and be glorified through their obedience.

The need for repentance

Here are some verses from the book of Haggai in the King James Version that speak about the need for repentance:

1. "Thus saith the Lord of hosts; Consider your ways." (Haggai 1:7)
2. "Go up to the mountain, and bring wood, and build the house; and I will take pleasure in it, and I will be glorified, saith the Lord." (Haggai 1:8)
3. "Ye looked for much, and, lo, it came to little; and when ye brought it home, I did blow upon it. Why? saith the Lord of hosts. Because of mine house that is waste, and ye run every man unto his own house." (Haggai 1:9)
4. "Therefore the heaven over you is stayed from dew, and the earth is stayed from her fruit." (Haggai 1:10)
5. "Consider now from this day and upward, from the four and twentieth day of the ninth month, even from the day that the foundation of the Lord's temple was laid, consider it." (Haggai 2:18)
6. "Is the seed yet in the barn? yea, as yet the vine, and the fig tree, and the pomegranate, and the olive tree, hath not brought forth: from this day will I bless you." (Haggai 2:19)

These verses speak about how the people of Israel had neglected to rebuild the temple, which was a sign of their lack of repentance and disobedience to God. The prophet Haggai urged them to reconsider their ways and rebuild the temple, promising that if they did, God would bless them. The verses also suggest that the lack of obedience had resulted in a lack of blessings, such as a lack of dew and fruit. The call to repentance is a major theme throughout the book of Haggai.

The sovereignty and faithfulness of God

Here are some verses from Haggai that speak of the sovereignty and faithfulness of God in the KJV translation:

1. "For thus saith the Lord of hosts; Yet once, it is a little while, and I will shake the heavens, and the earth, and the sea, and the dry land;" (Haggai 2:6)
2. "The silver is mine, and the gold is mine, saith the Lord of hosts." (Haggai 2:8)
3. "And I will shake all nations, and the desire of all nations shall come: and I will fill this house with glory, saith the Lord of hosts." (Haggai 2:7)
4. "According to the word that I covenanted with you when ye came out of Egypt, so my spirit remaineth among you: fear ye not." (Haggai 2:5)
5. "Thus saith the Lord of hosts; Consider your ways." (Haggai 1:7)
6. "And the Lord stirred up the spirit of Zerubbabel the son of Shealtiel, governor of Judah, and the spirit of Joshua the son of Josedech, the high priest, and the spirit of all the remnant of the people; and they came and did work in the house of the Lord of hosts, their God," (Haggai 1:14)
7. "The glory of this latter house shall be greater than of the former, saith the Lord of hosts: and in this place will I give peace, saith the Lord of hosts." (Haggai 2:9)

These verses speak to the power and sovereignty of God over all things, including the material wealth and resources of the earth. They also emphasize the faithfulness of God to his promises, reminding the people of the covenant made with them when they came out of Egypt. God is portrayed as a God who stirs up the spirits of the people to action, inspiring them to do the work necessary to rebuild the temple. Ultimately, the prophecy of Haggai speaks of the glory of the Lord and the peace that will come through his presence in the temple.

The promise of future glory

Here are some verses from the book of Haggai in the King James Version (KJV) that speak about the promise of future glory:

1. "The glory of this latter house shall be greater than of the former, saith the Lord of hosts: and in this place will I give peace, saith the Lord of hosts." - Haggai 2:9
2. "For thus saith the Lord of hosts; Yet once, it is a little while, and I will shake the heavens, and the earth, and the sea, and the dry land;" - Haggai 2:6
3. "The silver is mine, and the gold is mine, saith the Lord of hosts." - Haggai 2:8
4. "And I will shake all nations, and the desire of all nations shall come: and I will fill this house with glory, saith the Lord of hosts." - Haggai 2:7
5. "And I will overthrow the throne of kingdoms, and I will destroy the strength of the kingdoms of the heathen; and I will overthrow the chariots, and those that ride in them; and the horses and their riders shall come down, every one by the sword of his brother." - Haggai 2:22

These verses speak about God's promise to restore His people and His Temple after a period of destruction and exile. The promise of future glory is highlighted in these verses, where God promises to give peace, shake the heavens and earth, and fill the house with glory. He also promises to overthrow the kingdoms of the heathen and bring down those who oppress His people. Through these promises, God assures His people of His sovereignty and faithfulness, and encourages them to trust in Him for their future.

The role of the prophet

Here are some verses from the book of Haggai that speak about the role of the prophet, using the King James Version of the Bible:

1. "Then spake Haggai the LORD'S messenger in the LORD'S message unto the people, saying, I am with you, saith the LORD." (Haggai 1:13)
2. "And the LORD stirred up the spirit of Zerubbabel the son of Shealtiel, governor of Judah, and the spirit of Joshua the son of Josedech, the high priest, and the spirit of all the remnant of the people; and they came and did work in the house of the LORD of hosts, their God." (Haggai 1:14)
3. "In that day, saith the LORD of hosts, will I take thee, O Zerubbabel, my servant, the son of Shealtiel, saith the LORD, and will make thee as a signet: for I have chosen thee, saith the LORD of hosts." (Haggai 2:23)

In these verses, we see that Haggai was a messenger of the Lord who spoke to the people on behalf of God. He encouraged the people to rebuild the temple and reminded them of God's presence with them. The prophet also played a role in stirring up the spirits of the leaders and the people to do the work of God. Finally, we see that Haggai prophesied about the future glory of Zerubbabel, who would be chosen by God to be a signet, or a symbol of God's authority and power.

17

Zechariah - Minor Prophet (520-518 BC)

The name “Zechariah” means “Yahweh has remembered” in Hebrew.

Zechariah was a prophet in the Hebrew Bible and the author of the Book of Zechariah, which is the eleventh of the twelve minor prophets. He lived during the time of the Persian Empire and was among those who returned to Jerusalem from Babylonian exile. His book contains visions and messages from God that were intended to encourage the people to rebuild the temple and to return to the worship of God.

Zechariah was likely born in Babylon, where he lived during the Jewish exile. He was part of the community of exiles who returned to Jerusalem under the leadership of Zerubbabel and Joshua, the high priest. He was a contemporary of the prophet Haggai, and both of their books are focused on the rebuilding of the temple.

The historical and cultural context in which Zechariah lived was one of restoration and rebuilding. The Jews had returned from exile and were attempting to rebuild their lives and their city. They faced opposition from neighboring peoples, and the rebuilding of the temple had been stalled for many years. Zechariah’s messages of encouragement and hope were meant to inspire the people to continue with the work of rebuilding the temple and to trust in God’s faithfulness.

Historical and Cultural Context

The prophet Zechariah lived during the time of the rebuilding of the temple in Jerusalem after the Babylonian exile. This was a time of great political and social upheaval as the Jewish people attempted to re-establish their homeland and identity. The Persian Empire had conquered the Babylonians and allowed the Jews to return to Jerusalem and rebuild their temple, but they still faced opposition and challenges from neighboring peoples.

Zechariah's prophetic ministry was focused on encouraging the Jewish people to complete the rebuilding of the temple and to recommit themselves to the covenant with God. He also spoke of the coming of the Messiah and the establishment of God's kingdom on earth, providing hope and vision for the future. Zechariah's prophecies were written in the context of this historical and cultural background.

Importance

The book of Zechariah is important for several reasons. Firstly, it provides a historical account of the rebuilding of the temple in Jerusalem after the Babylonian exile, as well as the restoration of Jewish worship and religious practices. Secondly, the book contains numerous prophecies that point to the coming of the Messiah and the establishment of God's kingdom. These prophecies are referenced and fulfilled in the New Testament, making Zechariah an important part of the Christian canon.

Thirdly, Zechariah is notable for its use of apocalyptic imagery and themes, which are explored in depth in the latter half of the book. This makes Zechariah a unique contribution to the prophetic literature of the Old Testament. Finally, the book of Zechariah emphasizes the importance of faith, obedience, and repentance in the life of God's people, making it a valuable source of wisdom and guidance for believers of all generations.

Structure and organization

The book of Zechariah is structured into two main parts:

1. Chapters 1-8: These chapters consist of a series of eight visions that the prophet receives from the Lord. Each vision involves symbolic imagery and emphasizes God's sovereignty, faithfulness, and plan for the restoration of Jerusalem and the temple.
2. Chapters 9-14: These chapters contain a series of oracles and prophecies that emphasize the coming of a future messianic age, including the arrival of a righteous king who will bring peace and prosperity to Israel.

Overall, the book of Zechariah is organized thematically around the themes of God's sovereignty, judgment and restoration, and the coming of a future messianic age.

Major themes

The book of Zechariah has several major themes, including:

1. The coming of the Messiah: Zechariah prophesies about the coming of a king who will bring salvation to God's people.
2. The rebuilding of the temple: After the Babylonian exile, the temple in Jerusalem had been destroyed. Zechariah encourages the rebuilding of the temple and speaks of its future glory.
3. Repentance and restoration: Zechariah calls the people of Judah to repentance and promises God's restoration and blessing if they return to him.
4. The day of the Lord: Zechariah speaks of the day when God will judge the nations and establish his kingdom on earth.
5. The role of the prophet: Zechariah portrays himself as a watchman who delivers God's messages to the people.

Overall, the book of Zechariah provides a message of hope and encouragement to God's people, as they seek to rebuild their lives and their relationship with God after the devastation of the Babylonian exile.

The coming of the Messiah

Here are some verses in Zechariah that speak about the coming of the Messiah:

1. "Rejoice greatly, O daughter of Zion! Shout aloud, O daughter of Jerusalem! Behold, your king is coming to you; righteous and having salvation is he, humble and mounted on a donkey, on a colt, the foal of a donkey." (Zechariah 9:9)
2. "And I will pour out on the house of David and the inhabitants of Jerusalem a spirit of grace and pleas for mercy, so that, when they look on me, on him whom they have pierced, they shall mourn for him, as one mourns for an only child, and weep bitterly over him, as one weeps over a firstborn." (Zechariah 12:10)
3. "Awake, O sword, against my shepherd, against the man who stands next to me," declares the Lord of hosts. "Strike the shepherd, and the sheep will be scattered; I will turn my hand against the little ones." (Zechariah 13:7)
4. "On that day there shall be a fountain opened for the house of David and the inhabitants of Jerusalem, to cleanse them from sin and uncleanness." (Zechariah 13:1)

These verses speak of the coming of the Messiah as a righteous and humble king who will ride on a donkey. They also speak of his death and the mourning that will follow, as well as the fountain that will be opened for cleansing from sin.

The rebuilding of the temple

Here are some verses from the book of Zechariah in the King James Version (KJV) that mention the rebuilding of the temple:

1. "Thus speaketh the LORD of hosts, saying, This people say, The time is not come, the time that the LORD'S house should be built." - Zechariah 1:2
2. "Therefore thus saith the LORD; I am returned to Jerusalem with mercies: my house shall be built in it, saith the LORD of hosts, and a line shall be stretched forth upon Jerusalem." - Zechariah 1:16
3. "Thus saith the LORD of hosts; Behold, I will save my people from the east country, and from the west country; And I will bring them, and they shall dwell in the midst of Jerusalem: and they shall be my people, and I will be their God, in truth and in righteousness." - Zechariah 8:7-8
4. "And the LORD shall inherit Judah his portion in the holy land, and shall choose Jerusalem again." - Zechariah 2:12
5. "And speak unto him, saying, Thus speaketh the LORD of hosts, saying, Behold the man whose name is The BRANCH; and he shall grow up out of his place, and he shall build the temple of the LORD:" - Zechariah 6:12

These verses indicate that God desired the rebuilding of the temple in Jerusalem and promised to be with his people as they undertook this task. The temple was seen as a symbol of God's presence among his people, and the rebuilding of it was an important step in the restoration of Israel. Additionally, the promise of the coming Messiah who would build the temple further emphasizes the significance of this task in the plan of God for his people.

Repentance and restoration

Here are some verses from Zechariah about repentance and restoration, using the KJV translation:

- "Therefore say thou unto them, Thus saith the Lord of hosts; Turn ye unto me, saith the Lord of hosts, and I will turn unto you, saith the Lord of hosts." (Zechariah 1:3)
- "Therefore thus saith the Lord; I am returned to Jerusalem with mercies: my house shall be built in it, saith the Lord of hosts, and a line shall be stretched forth upon Jerusalem." (Zechariah 1:16)
- "Thus saith the Lord of hosts; Behold, I will save my people from the east country, and from the west country;" (Zechariah 8:7)
- "And many nations shall be joined to the Lord in that day, and shall be my people: and I will dwell in the midst of thee, and thou shalt know that the Lord of hosts hath sent me unto thee." (Zechariah 2:11)
- "In that day shall the Lord defend the inhabitants of Jerusalem; and he that is feeble among them at that day shall be as David; and the house of David shall be as God, as the angel of the Lord before them." (Zechariah 12:8)

These verses speak of the need for repentance and turning back to the Lord, as well as the promise of restoration and salvation for God's people. They also speak of the ultimate fulfillment of these promises in the coming of the Messiah and the establishment of his kingdom.

The day of the Lord

1. "Behold, the day of the Lord cometh, and thy spoil shall be divided in the midst of thee." (Zechariah 14:1)
2. "And it shall come to pass in that day, saith the Lord of hosts, that I will cut off the names of the idols out of the land, and they shall no more be remembered: and also I will cause the prophets and the unclean spirit to pass out of the land." (Zechariah 13:2)
3. "And I will pour upon the house of David, and upon the inhabitants of Jerusalem, the spirit of grace and of supplications: and they shall look upon me whom they have pierced, and they shall mourn for him, as one mourneth for his only son, and shall be in bitterness for him, as one that

is in bitterness for his firstborn." (Zechariah 12:10)

4. "In that day shall the Lord defend the inhabitants of Jerusalem; and he that is feeble among them at that day shall be as David; and the house of David shall be as God, as the angel of the Lord before them." (Zechariah 12:8)
5. "And it shall come to pass in that day, that I will seek to destroy all the nations that come against Jerusalem." (Zechariah 12:9)

These verses in Zechariah speak about the "day of the Lord," which is a time of judgment and reckoning. The day of the Lord is a theme found throughout the prophetic books of the Old Testament, and it is a day when God will intervene in human history to judge the wicked and deliver the righteous. The verses in Zechariah describe the destruction of the nations that come against Jerusalem, the pouring out of God's spirit on the people, and the mourning for the one whom they have pierced. These verses also speak of the defense of the inhabitants of Jerusalem and the transformation of the house of David.

The role of the prophet

There are several verses in the book of Zechariah that speak to the role of the prophet:

1. "Then the angel who talked with me returned and woke me up, like someone awakened from sleep. He asked me, 'What do you see?' I answered, 'I see a solid gold lampstand with a bowl at the top and seven lamps on it, with seven channels to the lamps.'" - Zechariah 4:1-2
2. "This is what the Lord Almighty said: 'Administer true justice; show mercy and compassion to one another. Do not oppress the widow or the fatherless, the foreigner or the poor. Do not plot evil against each other.'" - Zechariah 7:9-10
3. "I will strengthen Judah and save the tribes of Joseph. I will restore them because I have compassion on them. They will be as though I had not

> rejected them, for I am the Lord their God and I will answer them. The Ephraimites will become like warriors, and their hearts will be glad as with wine. Their children will see it and be joyful; their hearts will rejoice in the Lord." - Zechariah 10:6-7

These verses demonstrate that Zechariah was a prophet who received divine visions and messages from the Lord, and was tasked with communicating them to the people of Israel. He was also called to encourage the people to live justly, showing mercy and compassion to one another, and not to oppress the marginalized. Finally, he spoke of the restoration of the nation of Israel, a theme that is common throughout the prophetic books of the Old Testament.

18

Malachi - Minor Prophet (430-400 BC)

Malachi is one of the twelve minor prophets of the Old Testament. Very little is known about the personal background of Malachi, and there is some debate over the time period in which he prophesied. Some scholars suggest that Malachi ministered during the reign of Ezra, Nehemiah, or possibly Artaxerxes II, while others believe he prophesied after the rebuilding of the temple in Jerusalem in 516 BC.

Malachi's prophetic message is directed primarily at the Jewish people who had returned to Judah following the Babylonian exile. He addresses issues of the priesthood, the temple, and the people's lack of faithfulness to God. Malachi's prophecies include both words of warning and words of comfort and hope, emphasizing the importance of repentance and the promise of God's faithfulness to his people. The book of Malachi contains only four chapters, making it the shortest book among the twelve minor prophets.

Historical and Cultural Context

The prophet Malachi lived during a time when the Jewish people had returned to Jerusalem from Babylonian exile and were struggling to rebuild their lives and restore their faith in God. The people were faced with a variety of challenges, including economic hardship, social injustice, and spiritual apathy. Malachi's prophecies were directed at these issues, calling the people to repentance, obedience, and faithfulness to God.

Historically, Malachi lived during the Persian period of Jewish history, when the Jews were under the rule of the Persian Empire. This was a time of relative peace and stability, but also of cultural and religious assimilation, as the Jews were influenced by Persian culture and religion. Malachi's prophecies address these issues as well, calling the people to reject idolatry and to remain faithful to the God of their ancestors.

Importance

The book of Malachi is the last book of the Old Testament, and it contains a powerful message of repentance and hope. Its importance lies in its prophetic call for the people of Israel to turn back to God and to live according to his ways. The book is also significant in that it contains some of the clearest prophecies of the coming of John the Baptist and the Messiah.

Malachi wrote during a time when the people of Israel were living in a state of spiritual decline. The rebuilding of the temple had been completed, but the people had become apathetic in their worship and had turned away from God. They were practicing religious rituals without true devotion, and their hearts were far from God. Malachi's message called them to repentance and to return to a faithful relationship with God.

The book of Malachi also speaks to the importance of faithfulness and obedience to God's laws. Malachi rebukes the priests for their lack of integrity and for their failure to teach the people God's ways. He reminds the people that God desires sincere worship and obedience, not just empty religious rituals. Malachi's message is a call to live a life of faithfulness to God and to seek first his kingdom and his righteousness.

Structure and organization

The book of Malachi consists of four chapters, making it the shortest book among the twelve minor prophets in the Old Testament. The structure of the book can be divided into six sections:

1. The introduction (1:1)
2. God's love for Israel (1:2–5)
3. The priests' neglect of their duties (1:6–2:9)
4. Israel's unfaithfulness to God (2:10–16)
5. The coming day of judgment (2:17–4:3)
6. The call to repentance (4:4–6)

Each section is connected to the overall theme of the book, which is a call for Israel to repent and turn back to God.

Major Themes

The book of Malachi touches on several themes, including:

1. Faithfulness and Unfaithfulness: The book highlights God's faithfulness to His people, even when they have been unfaithful to Him. It also calls for the people to remain faithful to God and His commandments.
2. The Priests: Malachi addresses the corrupt behavior of the priests, who were not fulfilling their duties properly and were leading the people astray.
3. Justice: Malachi speaks out against social injustice and oppression, calling for the people to treat one another fairly and justly.
4. The Day of the Lord: The book also looks forward to the coming of the Messiah and the Day of the Lord, when God will judge the wicked and reward the righteous.
5. Repentance: Malachi encourages the people to repent and turn back to God, promising that He will forgive and restore them if they do so.

Overall, the book of Malachi emphasizes the importance of faithfulness, justice, and repentance in the relationship between God and His people. It also speaks to the hope and promise of the coming of the Messiah and the ultimate judgment and restoration that will come with the Day of the Lord.

Faithfulness and Unfaithfulness

There are several verses in the book of Malachi that touch on the themes of faithfulness and unfaithfulness:

1. Malachi 1:6 - "A son honoureth his father, and a servant his master: if then I be a father, where is mine honour? and if I be a master, where is my fear? saith the Lord of hosts unto you, O priests, that despise my name. And ye say, Wherein have we despised thy name?"
2. Malachi 1:14 - "But cursed be the deceiver, which hath in his flock a male, and voweth, and sacrificeth unto the Lord a corrupt thing: for I am a great King, saith the Lord of hosts, and my name is dreadful among the heathen."
3. Malachi 2:7 - "For the priest's lips should keep knowledge, and they should seek the law at his mouth: for he is the messenger of the Lord of hosts."
4. Malachi 2:16 - "For the Lord, the God of Israel, saith that he hateth putting away: for one covereth violence with his garment, saith the Lord of hosts: therefore take heed to your spirit, that ye deal not treacherously."
5. Malachi 3:6 - "For I am the Lord, I change not; therefore ye sons of Jacob are not consumed."
6. Malachi 3:8-9 - "Will a man rob God? Yet ye have robbed me. But ye say, Wherein have we robbed thee? In tithes and offerings. Ye are cursed with a curse: for ye have robbed me, even this whole nation."
7. Malachi 4:6 - "And he shall turn the heart of the fathers to the children, and the heart of the children to their fathers, lest I come and smite the earth with a curse."

These verses highlight the importance of faithfulness to God and his laws, and the consequences of unfaithfulness and disobedience. The book of Malachi emphasizes the need for repentance and obedience, and the promise of God's faithfulness to those who follow him.

The Priests

Here are some verses from the book of Malachi regarding the priests in the KJV translation:

- Malachi 1:6 - "A son honoureth his father, and a servant his master: if then I be a father, where is mine honour? and if I be a master, where is my fear? saith the Lord of hosts unto you, O priests, that despise my name. And ye say, Wherein have we despised thy name?"
- Malachi 2:7 - "For the priest's lips should keep knowledge, and they should seek the law at his mouth: for he is the messenger of the Lord of hosts."
- Malachi 2:8 - "But ye are departed out of the way; ye have caused many to stumble at the law; ye have corrupted the covenant of Levi, saith the Lord of hosts."
- Malachi 2:9 - "Therefore have I also made you contemptible and base before all the people, according as ye have not kept my ways, but have been partial in the law."
- Malachi 2:13-14 - "And this have ye done again, covering the altar of the Lord with tears, with weeping, and with crying out, insomuch that he regardeth not the offering any more, or receiveth it with good will at your hand. Yet ye say, Wherefore? Because the Lord hath been witness between thee and the wife of thy youth, against whom thou hast dealt treacherously: yet is she thy companion, and the wife of thy covenant."
- Malachi 2:17 - "Ye have wearied the Lord with your words. Yet ye say, Wherein have we wearied him? When ye say, Every one that doeth evil is good in the sight of the Lord, and he delighteth in them; or, Where is the God of judgment?"

These verses address the behavior and responsibilities of the priests in Israel during Malachi's time. The Lord rebukes the priests for dishonoring His name, causing others to stumble at the law, and being partial in their application of it. The priests are also rebuked for their treacherous treatment of their wives and for regarding evil as good. Overall, the book of Malachi emphasizes the importance of faithfulness, obedience, and reverence for God.

Justice

Here are some verses from Malachi in the King James Version (KJV) that speak about justice:

1. Malachi 2:17 - "Ye have wearied the Lord with your words. Yet ye say, Wherein have we wearied him? When ye say, Every one that doeth evil is good in the sight of the Lord, and he delighteth in them; or, Where is the God of judgment?"
2. Malachi 3:5 - "And I will come near to you to judgment; and I will be a swift witness against the sorcerers, and against the adulterers, and against false swearers, and against those that oppress the hireling in his wages, the widow, and the fatherless, and that turn aside the stranger from his right, and fear not me, saith the Lord of hosts."
3. Malachi 3:16-18 - "Then they that feared the Lord spake often one to another: and the Lord hearkened, and heard it, and a book of remembrance was written before him for them that feared the Lord, and that thought upon his name. And they shall be mine, saith the Lord of hosts, in that day when I make up my jewels; and I will spare them, as a man spareth his own son that serveth him. Then shall ye return, and discern between the righteous and the wicked, between him that serveth God and him that serveth him not."
4. Malachi 4:1-2 - "For, behold, the day cometh, that shall burn as an oven; and all the proud, yea, and all that do wickedly, shall be stubble: and the day that cometh shall burn them up, saith the Lord of hosts, that it shall leave them neither root nor branch. But unto you that fear my name shall the Sun of righteousness arise with healing in his wings; and ye shall go forth, and grow up as calves of the stall."

These verses show that God is a God of justice who will judge those who oppress and do wickedness. Those who fear the Lord and serve Him will be spared on the day of judgment and will be blessed with healing and growth. The book of Malachi emphasizes the importance of righteousness and faithfulness in the eyes of God.

The Day of the Lord

Here are some verses from Malachi that relate to the Day of the Lord:

1. "For behold, the day cometh, that shall burn as an oven; and all the proud, yea, and all that do wickedly, shall be stubble: and the day that cometh shall burn them up, saith the Lord of hosts, that it shall leave them neither root nor branch." (Malachi 4:1)
2. "But who may abide the day of his coming? and who shall stand when he appeareth? for he is like a refiner's fire, and like fullers' soap." (Malachi 3:2)
3. "Behold, I will send you Elijah the prophet before the coming of the great and dreadful day of the Lord:" (Malachi 4:5)
4. "For, behold, the day cometh, that shall burn as an oven; and all the proud, yea, and all that do wickedly, shall be stubble: and the day that cometh shall burn them up, saith the Lord of hosts, that it shall leave them neither root nor branch." (Malachi 4:1)
5. "And ye shall tread down the wicked; for they shall be ashes under the soles of your feet in the day that I shall do this, saith the Lord of hosts." (Malachi 4:3)

These verses describe the coming Day of the Lord, which will be a time of judgment and punishment for the wicked. The Lord will send Elijah the prophet before this day, and the proud and wicked will be burned up like stubble. However, those who are righteous will tread down the wicked and will be triumphant in the day of the Lord. These verses emphasize the importance of living a righteous life and being prepared for the coming of the Lord.

Repentance

Here are some verses of repentance in the book of Malachi (KJV):

1. “If I am a master, where is my fear? says the LORD of hosts to you, O priests, who despise my name. But you say, ‘How have we despised your name?’ By offering polluted food upon my altar. But you say, ‘How have we polluted you?’ By saying that the LORD’s table may be despised. When you offer blind animals in sacrifice, is that not evil? And when you offer those that are lame or sick, is that not evil? Present that to your governor; will he accept you or show you favor? says the LORD of hosts.” (Malachi 1:6–8)
2. “But who can endure the day of his coming, and who can stand when he appears? For he is like a refiner’s fire and like fullers’ soap. He will sit as a refiner and purifier of silver, and he will purify the sons of Levi and refine them like gold and silver, and they will bring offerings in righteousness to the LORD.” (Malachi 3:2–3)
3. “Will man rob God? Yet you are robbing me. But you say, ‘How have we robbed you?’ In your tithes and contributions. You are cursed with a curse, for you are robbing me, the whole nation of you. Bring the full tithe into the storehouse, that there may be food in my house. And thereby put me to the test, says the LORD of hosts, if I will not open the windows of heaven for you and pour down for you a blessing until there is no more need.” (Malachi 3:8–10)

19

Sources for Further Study

Here are some sources for further study on the prophets and their respective books:

1. The Bible (various translations) The primary source for studying the prophets is the Bible itself. The prophetic books are part of the Old Testament and can be found in most versions of the Bible.
2. Commentaries Commentaries are books that provide in-depth analysis and interpretation of biblical texts. They can be a valuable resource for gaining a deeper understanding of the prophetic books. Some popular commentaries on the prophets include:

- The Expositor's Bible Commentary
- The New International Commentary on the Old Testament
- The Tyndale Old Testament Commentaries
- RSTNE SCRIPTURES & STUDY GUIDE

1. Study Bibles Study Bibles provide notes and commentary alongside the biblical text, making it easier to understand the context and meaning of the prophets. Some popular study Bibles that include the prophetic books are:

- The ESV Study Bible
- The NIV Study Bible
- The Life Application Study Bible

1. Online Resources There are many online resources available for studying the prophets, including:

- BibleGateway.com: a website that provides access to multiple translations of the Bible and allows for easy searching of specific passages.
- BlueLetterBible.org: a website that provides access to multiple translations of the Bible as well as tools for in-depth study, including commentaries and dictionaries.
- Bible.org: a website that provides free access to many resources, including commentaries and articles on the prophetic books.
- https://rstne.com/pages/copy-of-index-rstne-8th-edition-online

Printed in Great Britain
by Amazon